Gothic Kernow

Anthem Studies in Gothic Literature

Anthem Studies in Gothic Literature incorporates a broad range of titles that undertake rigorous, multi-disciplinary and original scholarship in the domain of Gothic Studies and respond, where possible, to existing classroom/module needs. The series aims to foster innovative international scholarship that interrogates established ideas in this rapidly growing field, to broaden critical and theoretical discussion among scholars and students, and to enhance the nature and availability of existing scholarly resources.

Gothic Kernow

Cornwall as Strange Fiction

Tanya Krzywinska and Ruth Heholt

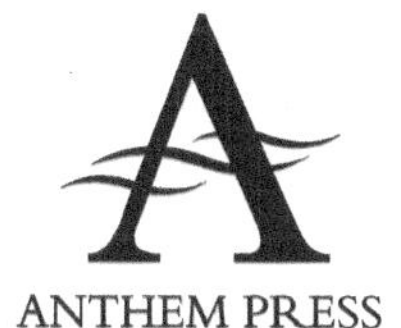

ANTHEM PRESS

Anthem Press
An imprint of Wimbledon Publishing Company
www.anthempress.com

This edition first published in UK and USA 2022
by ANTHEM PRESS
75–76 Blackfriars Road, London SE1 8HA, UK
or PO Box 9779, London SW19 7ZG, UK
and
244 Madison Ave #116, New York, NY 10016, USA

British Library Cataloguing-in-Publication Data
A catalogue record for this book is available from the British Library.

Library of Congress Control Number: 2021951100

ISBN-13: 978-1-78527-906-5 (Pbk)
ISBN-10: 1-78527-906-8 (Pbk)

Cover credit: 'Mansion Gothic Kernow', Tanya Krzywinska

This title is also available as an e-book.

CONTENTS

INTRODUCTION

Cornwall is the hidden heart of the Gothic. *Gothic Kernow: Cornwall as Strange Fiction* focuses on written and visual culture that is made in, or made about, Cornwall. We argue that Cornwall (known as 'Kernow' in the Cornish language) has a special relationship with Gothic, that has been largely overlooked in the literature on regional Gothic. We argue that Cornwall has been present as a force since the inception of the Gothic as a mode and that it is also central to the more recently identified Folk Horror genre. This kinship with both the Gothic and Folk Horror has been produced and reinforced through a rich culture of myth and magic that has been quickened by the region's geographical location and landscape.

Cornwall is saturated in mythology and folklore. From the deep-sea monster Morgawr, who is said to be sighted sometimes off Falmouth Bay, to the Cornish little people, the Knockers who dwell in the deep mines. From the Cornish cunning folk to witches to the Cornish pellars, and the ghosts, faeries, and piskies who inhabit the rugged and isolated landscapes, Cornwall is steeped in magic, mystery, and lore and has always provided a space for the Gothic. Cornwall is no stranger to darkness and loss. The last native language speaker of Cornish, Dolly Pentreath was lost as early as 1777 and the 'Great Migration' of the 1850s saw nearly a third of Cornwall's population move away from Cornwall as the mining and fishing industries declined. And it is from these times of loss and decay that both the Romantic and the Gothic find their creative expressions. This period of decline for Cornwall coincided with the mid to late Victorian folklore revival and there was a resurrection of the Cornish association with myths, legends, and lore. Alfred Tennyson's very popular cycle of poems, *Idylls of the King*, began in 1859 (concluding in 1885) and cemented the Arthurian legends to the (now) ruined castle of Tintagel. As a part of the folklore revival, two prominent Cornish nineteenth folklorists began collecting tales (sometimes known as drolls when associated with Cornwall), William Bottrell (1816–1881) and Robert Hunt (1807–1887). The tales Bottrell and Hunt collected are often dark, with ghouls and ghosts, accounts of real witches and pellars (Cornish for cunning person), 'knackers'

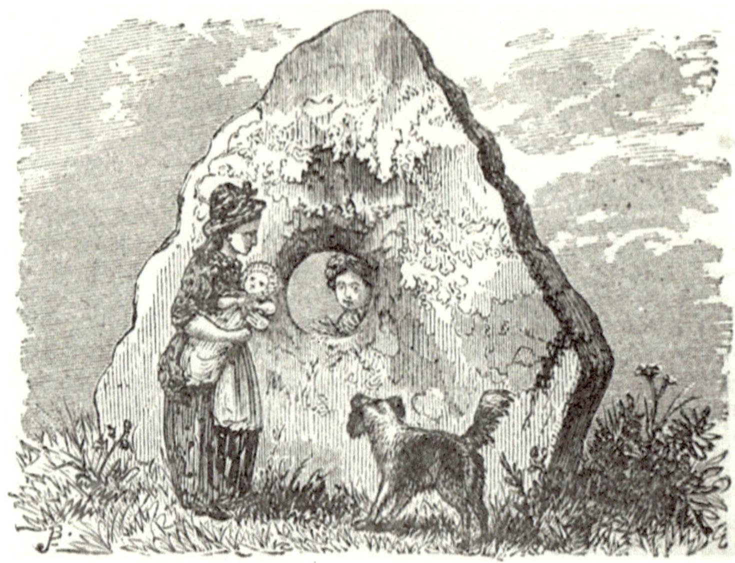

Figure 1 'Passing children through the Mên-an-Tol for healing'. Engraving from William Bottrell's *Traditions and Hearthside Stories of West Cornwall*, 1870. Out of copyright.

(or knockers) who live in the mines, piskies that lead the unaware off the path or conversely help with household chores, and the Bucca, a demonic faery-like figure with his two aspects.

> Penzance boys up in a tree,
> Looking as wisht as wisht can be;
> Newlyn buckas as strong as oak,
> Knocking them down at every poke. (Bottrell, 1890)

These tales have informed the more recent regional witch practice developed by Gemma Gary outlined in her book *Traditional Witchcraft: A Cornish Book of Ways* (2019).

At the same time as the folklore revival, the rise of the Victorian Gothic saw some of the most prominent of writers turn their attention to Cornwall. Wilkie Collins' based two novels in Cornwall: *Basil* (1852), and *The Dead Secret* (1856). In these tales, Collins envisions Cornwall as an old, wild, and primitive place of lawlessness and desire. Bram Stoker's *The Jewel of the Seven Stars* (1903), and Arthur Conan Doyle's short Sherlock Holmes story 'The Adventure of the Devil's Foot' (1910) both associate Cornwall with the exotic, foreign, and

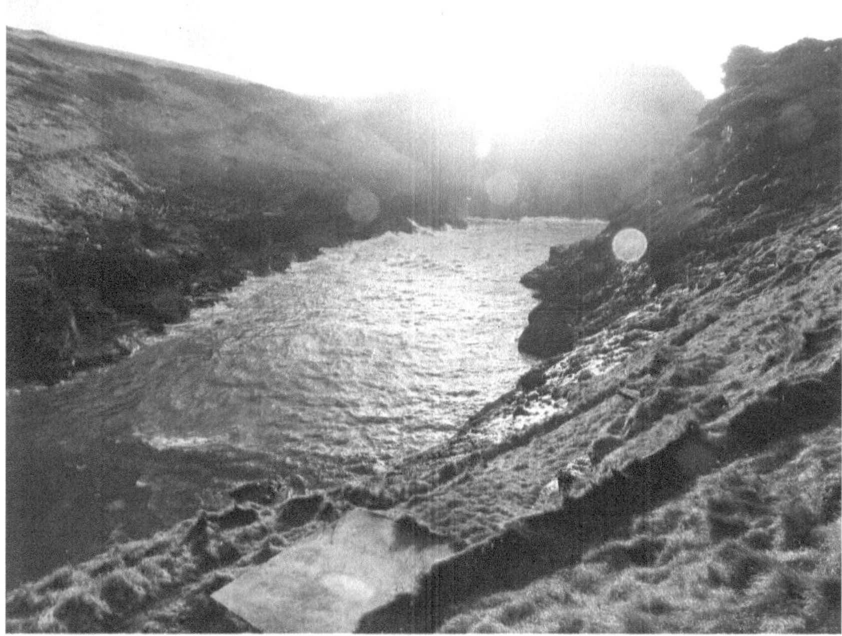

Figure 2 'Cornwall as Mystical Landscape: Boscastle Harbour'. Photograph by Tanya Krzywinska (2020).

the far away. (Bearing in mind that in the eighteenth and nineteenth centuries Cornwall was known as 'West Barbary', referencing the west coast of Africa, the Barbarian coast). Ghosts too figure prominently in the literature about Cornwall. Reverend Robert Stephen Hawker's 'The Botathen Ghost' (1867) being one of the most well-known. Many tales set in Cornwall exemplify what might be termed a 'sea Gothic'. This is evident in 1891 Sabine Baring Gould's 'In the Roar of the Sea' (1891) and Sir Arthur Quiller-Couch's 'The Roll Call of the Reef' (1895). Quiller-Couch was one of the most important Cornish writers and his tales epitomise the Gothic with fearful spectres, tragic mishaps, glowering landscapes, and a questioning of morality and sexuality. Over hundreds of years, Cornish Gothic has grown and flourished. The railway did not cross the Tamar from mainland England into Cornwall until 1859 enabling Cornwall to retain an air of mystery, uncivilization, and a throw-back to the 'old days'. The coming of the railway did not dispel this conception and indeed helped to cement these associations with a new touristic view of Cornwall as 'different'. A view of Cornwall as 'strange fiction' has been around for a very long time and, we argue, continues to be created today.

In 2021, as we write, the G7 summit of world leaders is due to convene in Carbis Bay in Cornwall. Where, one might ask, do world leaders meet to discuss things like the catastrophic climate crisis during a global pandemic? The answer it seems is, (to quote Joe Biden), 'the Cornwall'. According to Sky News, British prime minister Boris Johnson said, 'Two hundred years ago Cornwall's tin and copper mines were at the heart of the UK's industrial revolution and this summer Cornwall will again be the nucleus of great global change and advancement' (16 January 2021). But will it really? Can the centrist view really be skewed to advantage the regional way of seeing things? Cornwall was evidently chosen for a reason and it is perhaps no coincidence that, as *The Guardian* reports, Carbis Bay 'was the site of scenes in the fifth season of Poldark' (16 January 2021). It is therefore an *imagining* of Cornwall, a fictionalisation of place, that brings the summit here. Yet, within the imagining and romanticisation of Cornwall lurks that which is most dark: the climate crisis, world economic collapse, and of course COVID-19. Human life is shown therefore at its most fragile and under siege. The summit neatly signifies the hold that the uncanny Gothic doubling of Cornwall's landscapes has on the imagination.

In most of the reports about the 2021 G7 summit, the headlines are not of the convention's meeting in Britain or even England – but of Cornwall. This is not so surprising. Located at the far western tip of the British mainland, Cornwall's principality has been, and still is, contested. Largely untouched by the Roman, Danish, and Saxon invasions, Kernow retains its own Celtic language, much as the case with Wales, and many people still regard Cornwall as independent of 'England'. As our book demonstrates, this evocative and creatively generative separation plays an instrumental role in the region's place within the Gothic imagination.

With its rugged moors, towering cliffs, seductive coves, and expansive beaches, Cornwall has attracted the attention not only of world leaders but also of many artists and writers as well as filmmakers and photographers. As a peninsula as well as lying on the other side of the wide River Tamar and due to its many steep valleys, access from England proves difficult. Even in our mobile times, the sense of isolation persists, as evidenced in 2014 when a portion of the only railway line into Cornwall fell into the sea and took two months to repair. As such, isolation, a wild beauty, and an engrained mythic aura gives rise to what we might think of as the creative cult of Kernow – an imaginary place with a real referent to where an extraordinary diversity of artists have holidayed or resided in, using it as a spur to creativity. As such Kernow deserves our critical attention. It has inspired an incredible range of imaginative Gothic sensibilities that reach across diverse modes, materials, and forms, ranging from 'high' fine art through to popular and 'low' culture.

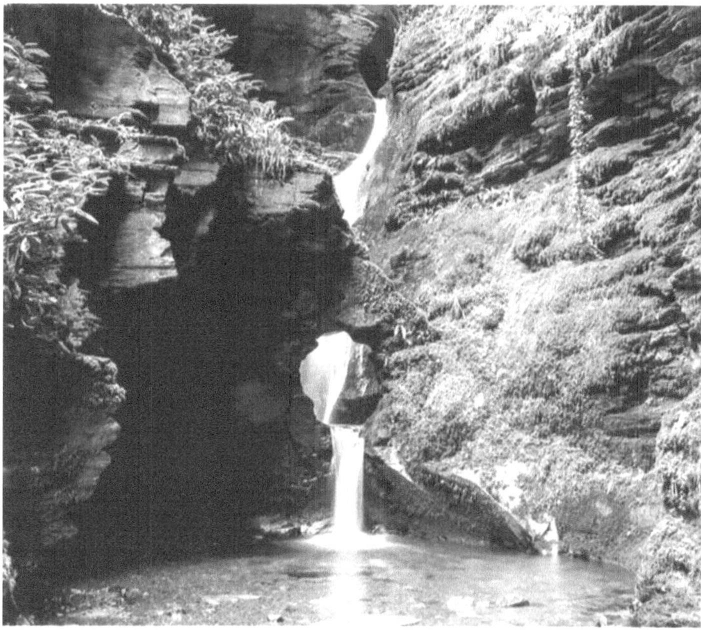

Figure 3 'Cornwall as Mystical Landscape: St Nectan's Glen'. Photograph by Tanya Krzywinska (2019).

In 1998, Avril Horner and Sue Zlosnik coined the term 'Cornish Gothic' in relation to the work of Daphne du Maurier (Horner and Zlosnik 1998). Since then, however, there have been few discussions of the distinctive types of Gothic engendered by cultural and imaginative re-creations of Cornwall, or of generative role for, and within, creative practice. Our book, *Gothic Kernow* argues that a persistent imaginative romance with the Cornish peninsular has produced a specific and distinctive set of Gothic fictions and creative outputs that mark an exciting new departure in the discussion of regional and media-specific Gothic studies. *Gothic Kernow* offers new insights into the relationships between place and Gothic. We aim to engender and encourage greater debate around what constitutes the Gothic through our argument that Cornwall continues to play a potent role in the landscape of regional Gothic. And, more than this, we advocate that Cornwall needs to be considered more fully as a major catalyst of and within the Gothic imagination.

Jarlath Killeen cites the Celtic fringes as 'Ireland, Scotland and Wales' (2009, 92–93). Cornwall is forgotten but it is the continued absence of Cornwall that defines it as a Gothic space. *Gothic Kernow* argues that Cornwall has a culturally acquired liminality, becoming a space of ambivalence, absence, excess, and

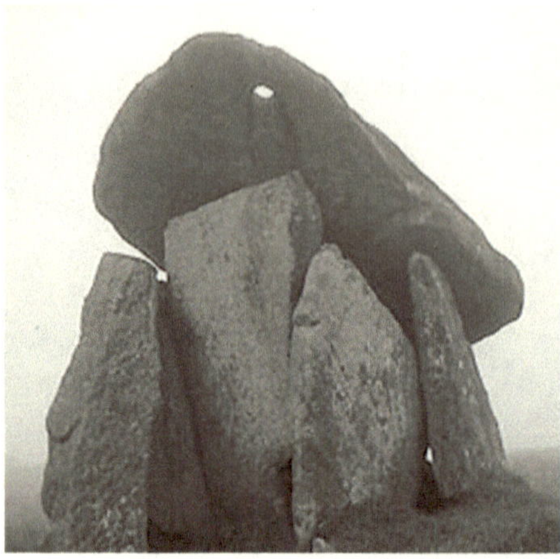

Figure 4 'Cornwall as Mystical Landscape: Trehevy Quoit'. Creative Commons.

loss. Cornwall is *too far away* and yet at the same time *too near* (at least for British scholars of Gothic). It has an excess in abundance: history, mythic non-history, outsider-rebel identity, uncanny light, crashing seas, and sublime sculptural stones. All this contributes to the construction of a dichotomous, intriguing space of fullness *and* lack. Kernow's past is largely undocumented; in prehistory, it was the richest of all realms, a land that yielded up magical, epoch-defining materials, and metals (tin, copper, china clay, gold, and, very recently, lithium). Kernow provides therefore a redolent mise en scène that supports all manner of imaginings, where we become free and at one with the untamed elements; the light is perfect, the morals loose, the repressed returns, and the deep magics of the old gods still hold sway. In a landscape punctuated by ancient standing stones and holy wells, tumultuous seas, and deep, dangerous mines, sold to tourists as a land of mists and magics, Cornwall is ripe terrain for the Gothic. The wealth of creative outputs and engagements it has produced attest to this. Daphne du Maurier, for instance, speaks of her romance with the region – 'Cornwall became my text' – in her pictorial memoir, *Enchanted Cornwall* (Du Maurier 1989, 7).

From Bodmin's ghosts and stalking beasts to the fey legends of the Knockers of the tin mines, and the mischievous Piskies and bad-tempered Spriggans of woods and the moors, Cornwall's folktales and myths are inextricably linked to place and landscape. The looming standing stones and the dark pits of the mines, the cliffs and coves, moors and surging seas sing-siren to the Gothic imagination. Beginning with the legendary temptation and trials of Jan Tregeagle, alongside tales of Cornish witches and pellars, Cornwall has ever had strong connections to mystery, magic, and legend, all providing fuel for wild imaginings. The stories that are told about Cornwall and its varied representations have the same permeable boundaries as the place itself. Films, novels, art, poetry, videogames, and all sorts of creative dreamings stem from the potential Gothic of Cornwall's terrain. Gothic is inherently a hybrid beast and Cornwall is a hybrid place, open to the sea and to what washes in with the tide. As Arthur Conan Doyle describes Cornwall: 'That long peninsula extending out into the ocean has caught all sorts of strange floating things, and has held them there in isolation' (*Through the Magic Door* 1907, 22). In sympathy with this, *Gothic Kernow* takes a transmedial and comparative approach, designed to show the textual and intertextual reach of space and place in the representational imagining of Cornwall.

Horner and Zlosnik argue that Daphne du Maurier's romance with Cornwall provides a means of focalising the author's Gothic engagement with issues of self and identity (1998). By contrast, this book widens the scope of their address. We look to the visual, the digital, and adaptation, to contemporary as well as traditional platforms, in pursuit of our argument that Kernow thrives as a dark economy for the creative imagination. No other work exists that has both a regional and transmedial focus on the 'Cornish Gothic'. In addition, we address the ways in which different platforms (i.e. novels, films, or painting) shape articulations of Gothic Kernow, alongside paying close attention to the threads of intertextual dialogue that weave patterns into the diversity.

In taking a transmedial approach to demonstrating the power of Gothic Kernow, we range quite freely across media platforms, fictional types, and creative practices. Beginning with du Maurier and moving through to the present day, we will tease out patterns of exchange across diverse forms that make up the cult of Kernow. Each chapter has a 'hub' text, artefact, or practice around which our comparative analyses hang. This structure allows us to move deftly between dark romances (*My Cousin Rachel*, 1951) and Folk Horror films such as *The Wicker Man* (1973), the magical paintings & writing of Ithell Colquhoun to those of artist-shaman Kate Walters, David Pinner's *Ritual* (2011 [1967]) to Susan Cooper's *Greenwitch* (1974) and Mark Jenkin's film *Bait* (2019).

As well as introducing readers to the characteristics of the region and those of its representation, throughout the course of the book, we set out our difference to other works on Cornish Gothic. Our comparative approach distinguishes our book from other works in this field, particularly Horner and Zlosnik's work on du Maurier (1998) or Amy Hale's work on Ithell Colquhoun (2004, 2012, 2020). Unlike other analyses, we centralise the region (Kernow), its myths and folk culture, landscape, and geology, and its role in the strange fictions that we address. As such, we do not foreground a single author, as is the case with Horner and Zlosnik, and Hale. Instead, we look across diverse authors, fictions, and platforms with an eye to recurring rhythms and counter rhythmical divergences. A further value of this book is its explicit demonstration that all the work and their creators, no matter what medium used or the nature of their relation to Gothic, are situated historically, culturally, and socially. Providing bedrock to our approach is the principle that Gothic Kernow is always situationally *produced* as a framework within which different aesthetic, psychological, and social agendas sit. As we will show, the texts and artefacts that we discuss are shaped by a confluence of medial formats and aesthetic concerns, political and social contexts, all filtering through the perceived magics, mysteries, and myths of Cornwall.

Chapter 1, 'Dark Romance and du Maurier's Gothic Kernow', looks at the way that Daphne du Maurier imagined a wild and romanticised Cornwall. Focusing on *My Cousin Rachel* but with reference to other du Maurier novels as well as some of the adaptations of her work, we argue that du Maurier's texts represent a crucially important moment in the creation of Cornwall as strange fiction and that they provide a legacy of imagining that is still being played out and recreated today. Animism is an insistent recurring rhythm that surfaces within representations of Kernow and it calls directly on the Cornish landscape – its moody sea, granite rocks, and standing stones, the chthonic qualities of deep mines, wild and remote moorland, and ever-changing light. Du Maurier herself animated the Cornish landscape and while we eschew the usual conjoining of her life and her texts, it is worth noting that perhaps she did not. Howsoever, these imaginings are by no means cast in benign light nor purely romanticised. And it is to this darker side of du Maurier's depictions of Cornwall that we turn, to who does and does not belong, to a landscape wild and unforgiving. Ending with the recent film *Bait*, the chapter traces du Maurier's legacy that reimagines Cornwall as a place of uncanny doubleness and as a space which can deceive, haunt, and echo its own imaginings.

Chapter 2, 'Supersensory Gothic Kernow: Magic, Mysticism, and the Esoteric Aesthetics of Emergence', examines the work of the artist and magician, Ithell Colquhoun (1906–1988). Core Gothic Studies concepts of otherness, animism, and the sublime provide the conceptual focus for the chapter's critical engagement with such work and its relationship with the Cornish Gothic. For the animist, nature and the cosmos are seen to possess soul or spiritual essence and forms. As we will show, the concept of animism is key to unlocking the values of Colquhoun's work and in the creation of a form of the Gothic where the body is synonymous with the landscape and the cosmos. We will refer to a range of her poetry, paintings, as well as the *roman noir*, *The Goose of Hermogenes* (1961), while in relation to Colquhoun's visual animism, as well as in her use of automatic methods, other visual

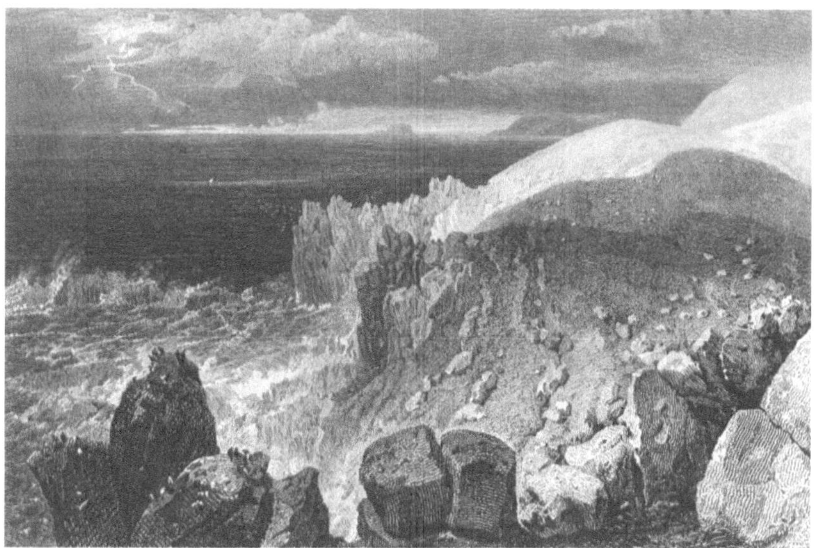

Figure 5 'Land's End. Image by J. M. W. Turner engraved by George Cooke, 1814'. By permission of Falmouth Art Gallery.

artists are considered. We look back to Turner's Cornish sketchbooks and move forward to touch on the works of poet Peter Redgrove and shamanic artist Kate Walters. Walters shares Colquhoun's use of generative and animistic techniques as a means of effecting transformation, repositioning women's experiences through both the physical and subtle body, the sacred and monstrous. Mobilising concepts such as the sublime, animism, and transformation allow this chapter to appraise the work of these artists in terms of a renewed definition of the Cornish Gothic that goes beyond a focus on popular culture or the work of du Maurier, as well as using Gothic as a means of providing fresh ways of looking at such work.

The focus of the third chapter, 'Strange Folk – Folk Horror Cultures, Ritual, and Witching Women', falls on a range of texts that collectively relate to the themes and format of Folk Horror. It has become a staple of renderings of Cornwall and therefore allies the region with pre-Christian, pagan religions and rites. These imaginings are indebted largely to Victorian revivals of old folk customs, as well as to du Maurier's son, Christian Browning's conviction that even within our own time 'legends still abound' (1992, viii). As we will show, Cornwall has its share of seemingly antique festival rituals, such as Padstow's 'Obby 'Oss, and other more recent inventions, such as Montol. These festivals echo imagined folk horror rituals of the sort that appear in the hub texts for this chapter: David Pinner's two novels, *Ritual* (1967), (on which the film, *The Wicker Man* is based albeit that the action in the film is transposed to Scotland), his more recent novel, *The Wicca Woman* (2014), and Susan Cooper's children's book *Greenwitch* (1973). In evaluating the role that ritual plays in the construction of Gothic Kernow, we argue that Folk Horror has its roots in Cornwall. As well as in textual sources, this can also be seen in the growth of real festivals as part of the region's appeal to dark tourism. Concentrating on the themes of ritual and sacrifice, this chapter moves on to examine sea rites and rituals in relation to the witching women of Cornwall. In arguing that Cornwall is one of the original sites for Folk Horror, we emphasise not only the darkness and the horror but also the possibilities given through the sea and the Cornish landscape of plenitude and life affirmation.

Throughout *Gothic Kernow*, we are intent on demonstrating how, as both an imagined, symbolic, and real space, Cornwall becomes the subject of Gothic concerns, particularly in terms of otherness, animism, and the sublime. Cornwall can be put on the Gothic map alongside Haiti, or H.P. Lovecraft and Stephen King country as real spaces that have a substantial and pervasive Gothic mythos attached to them. Most importantly, this book argues and demonstrates that Cornwall has been overlooked as a generative force in the shaping of the modern and contemporary Gothic and that Gothic Kernow needs to be considered as a powerful influence in the development of a Gothic grammar.

CHAPTER 1

DARK ROMANCE AND DU MAURIER'S GOTHIC KERNOW

Our first chapter provides the initial way into our topic through a focus on popular fictions that employ Gothic tropes and figurations in conjunction with a relationship to Cornwall. Our core intention here is to identify some of the major ways in which Cornwall has been represented in fictions that are well known and designed for consumption by a popular audience. In keeping with our intention to place a nodal hub text, or body of work, at the heart of each chapter and then proceed to a discussion of other related texts in a comparative and relational way, we have chosen Daphne du Maurier's novel of 1951, *My Cousin Rachel*. We have chosen this text as, although there is far less work on it than on *Rebecca*, interest in the novel has picked up recently including a big-budget 2017 adaptation. Further, the Cornish landscape plays a central role in this novel, with the rolling hills, cliff tops and seascapes representing the wild and untameable. Crucially for our interests, the landscape is juxtaposed with the cultivated garden-space which serves as its mirror or uncanny double. This (Italian) garden presents as a deceptively controllable place but, it is in fact the place that admits entry to the Other in the form of the foreign, unacceptable, sexually charged figure of Rachel. Embodied through Rachel, these features key into themes of identity, desire, animism, and ambiguity that provide the basis on which our investigation of Gothic Cornwall rests.

Du Maurier has often been associated with the Gothic by scholars, beginning with Avril Horner and Sue Zlosnik's *Daphne du Maurier: Writing, Identity and the Gothic Imagination* (1998). Such scholarship describes a biographical and more specifically autobiographical relationship between the author and the place. This chapter sidesteps this association and looks at the construction and imagining of the Gothic landscape itself in du Maurier's work and in the subsequent adaptations of her novels. As we will show, du Maurier's Cornish Gothic landscapes play a leading role in the construction of the Cornish landscape as a romantic terrain, a wilderness that is regularly employed as a means of promising both freedom and darkness. Throughout the book, we will examine the lure of fictionalising Cornwall as a space of seductive shadows. This chapter will therefore help to set up a supporting pillar of the book: that du Maurier's representations of Cornwall as a Gothic space have influenced and permeated many later popular cultural imaginings.

This chapter explores an 'ethics of imagining' of Kernow: as Other, dark, and threatening, and its uncanny twin the tourist imaginings of sublime and magical Cornwall. This idea of the 'doubling' of Cornwall runs throughout this chapter, whether it is twinning Cornwall with Italy in du Maurier's work, reconciling the beautiful and the harsher wild side of place and space, juxtaposing the cultivated sub-tropical garden spaces and the wilder seascapes, or the (sometimes disastrous) rift in the identification of the 'local' view of Cornwall with the romanticised 'tourist' vision. Beginning with an exploration of the work of one of the most iconic writers of Cornwall, Daphne du Maurier, we look at the creation of Cornwall as Gothic, strange fiction. We will argue that du Maurier's vision of Cornwall demonstrates an over-determination in the psycho-geographical positioning of Cornwall as at once peripheral and central. The 'view from Cornwall' presented in her work can be unreal, impossible to sustain, damagingly unworldly, unreliable, and dark. Yet this is often missed in discussions of her work that tend to concentrate on a romanticised identification with the landscape or with Cornwall's history. As Avril Horner and Sue Zlosnik argue, 'Her sense of identification with the peripheral culture of Cornwall may be seen as deriving from her attraction to its strangeness, the "otherness" of a landscape permeated by relics of the past and hints of beliefs alien to the seemingly rational world of the twentieth century' (1998, 68). This is the touristic view of both Cornwall and du Maurier's construction of it through her writing, where Cornwall is positioned as the Other. Du Maurier's work has undoubtedly inflected the way that Cornwall is seen, and it has had a lasting legacy on fictional and touristic imaginings of the county. This chapter explores the darker vision of Cornwall as presented in *My Cousin Rachel* and ends with reference to a film that draws on this legacy, *Bait* (2019). This recent film examines the dark, hard, gritty 'reality' of Kernow that is dramatically set against an economic and simulated vision of an imagined 'holiday idyll' Cornwall. These competing views lead from uneasy standoffs to disastrous results. Both *My Cousin Rachel* and *Bait* end in tragedy. In both texts, this comes about through a misreading, a misunderstanding, of what Cornwall is and what Cornwall is not. The 'inside' and the 'outside' viewpoints clash and both are evidentially skewed visions of reality. Du Maurier's vision of Cornwall incurs a recurring construction of place and space that might *appear* to be light and romanticised, all bright and breezy, but this comes loaded with a deep darkness. Through the seductive dramatic structures and tropes of romanticised fiction, Cornwall has led to some unintended consequences and legacies.

Du Maurier's Kernow: Regional Gothic and a Romantic Sensibility

In 2009, Catherine Spooner and Emma McEvoy, in their introduction to the section 'Gothic Locations' in *The Routledge Companion to Gothic*, begin an exploration of what they termed 'one of the newest areas of academic study of the Gothic: the exploration of location and of national tradition' (51). Since then, what is often termed 'regional Gothic' has become a rich area of study within the wider field of the growing scholarship around the 'Global Gothic', as in, for example, essays collected in *Globalgothic* (Byron, 2013). One of the concerns of these explorations is the relationship between what can be perceived as the centre, the peripheries and the margins. In the introduction to *Gothic Britain*, William Hughes notes that regional Gothic

> may be ensheathed in a national Gothic tradition, or in a Gothicised mode of writing about a certain country, but its central thrust is one of disrupting the simplicity of binary opposition. Its very acknowledgement of the margins as a cultural space with Gothic potential questions the relationships of power that balance the interplay of outsider and insider, educated and uneducated, traveller and resident. (2018, 15)

The regions and peripheries, through their very positioning as separated from the centre, engender their own unique manifestations of the Gothic. This new interest in the specific and sometimes discrete aesthetics of geographical margins and peripheries comes out of a long history of literary criticism that often dismissed work originating from these spaces. As Horner and Zlosnik note in relation to the reception of du Maurier's work, 'Regional writing has often been linked with limitation, a kind of parochial concern with matters specific to an area and an emphasis on "local colour" at the expense of the "universal" significance which traditional literary studies used to seek' (1998, 64–65). However, if, as Hughes notes, the Gothic disrupts, then attention paid to the regional can (in a very Gothic fashion) start to deconstruct and perhaps shatter any notion of the universal or central. Attention paid to the regional, the peripheral and the marginal begins a process of decentring that can lead to an uncomfortable (but perhaps fruitful) feeling of disorientation. As Jarlath Killeen claims,

> Gothic writers have always held the Colonial fringes to be particularly potent sources of horror for the English imagination, particularly those areas deemed part of the Celtic world. A view of England as surrounded, and concomitantly threatened, by the Celtic 'peripheries' transformed

> these regions into zones of radical indeterminacy and fertile sources for fears of ethnic infection and moral pollution. (2009, 3)

This positioning of 'England as surrounded', of course, places it in the embattled and threatened centre; terrors come from the borders and margins, fueling the regional Otherness of the Celtic fringe spaces such as Cornwall. Killeen however cites these Celtic peripheries as 'Ireland, Scotland and Wales' (2009, 92). In this discussion, (and often also elsewhere), Cornwall is missing. Shelley Trower also notes that work on the 'Celtic fringe' focuses on 'Ireland, Scotland and, to a lesser extent, Wales' (2015, 9). Despite its identification as part of the Celtic fringe, Cornwall is not mentioned. In the studies of the Celtic regions, Cornwall is left literally hanging off the edge, much as it seems to hang off the edge of England and the British mainland. This position inadvertently reflects the history of the Britons, those indigenous people who were pushed west to the edges of the land by invading Anglo-Saxons. Less 'known' than the other Celtic nations, Cornwall remains, at least to a certain extent, shrouded in prehistorical, cultural, and metaphorical darkness. This outsider, fringe status along with the sense that it is a land remaindered is, however, the very source of dark romance.

Cornwall is not quite like the other Celtic peripheries, conceptions of which formed a Romantic, Celtic Revival Movement during the nineteenth century. This movement harked back to the Romantic period that preceded and blended into the Gothic genre and placed great emphasis on the landscape. The Romantic view of the landscape tends, however, to be one of distance. The landscape is surveyed often by those who do not come from the region in question and who see the landscape as being 'over there', with their critical eye identifying 'otherness' and 'difference'. This is the Wordsworthian view of landscape – viewed from a height or a peak, with the mind interpreting the vista and gaining a personal sense of the sublime: in effect set apart and taking from the landscape rather than truly residing within it. Vijay Mishra cites the Romantic artist as being 'a God-like spectator, for whom nature exists via an all-pervading perceiver responsible both for its awesome splendor and its serene beauty' (2012, 289). This brings with it a comforting sense of control and superiority which does not equate with the Gothic sensibility that this book is concerned with. Yet the Romantic and the Gothic are never very far apart and indeed, even if we split the genres (which is not always possible), they are originally located during the same period. As Mishra says of the Gothic,

> Its frightening truth lay in its negation of the transcendental and healing principles of the Romantic sublime. [T]he Gothic subject finds no

> redeeming wanderer and embraces the demon within. The texts are nightmares from which one never recovers, as these nightmares signify mysteries which can be neither framed nor allegorized. (2012, 296)

Cornwall a nightmare? Perhaps not entirely, and the Gothic nightmare has a certain dark deliciousness. Du Maurier's imaginings of Cornwall are by no means all light and delight either; there is always something darker that resides within. The 'view from Cornwall' in du Maurier, as well as in later writings about Cornwall, often presents a vision that is underlaid, both actually and metaphorically, with the unforgiving, impenetrable blackness of granite. This granite – the fabric out of which the Cornish terrain is largely made – is leveraged to reinforce melodramatic themes of sexual transgression and desire, freedom, and determination and to feed the desire for vicarious adventure.

Ella Westland contends that Cornwall itself blends the Romantic and the Gothic genres. She says,

> By the 1790s it was no longer necessary to leave Britain in search of a rugged landscape which would inspire ecstasy, tranquility, sweet melancholy or Gothic horror, since artists had prepared enthusiasts to experience the serene and sublime in areas like the Lake District, the Scottish Highlands, the Wye Valley and the Isle of Wight. The transformation of Cornwall in the English imagination depended on rocky shores and surging seas taking their place with dark forests and snowy summits as approved sites for romantic sublimity. (1995, 154)

Over time, the locations of both the Romantic and the Gothic shifted from the Continent, coming (from an English point of view) 'home'. Du Maurier's fiction bridges the dark but narrow chasm between the Romantic and the Gothic, producing a Cornwall that is imaginatively invested with both. And while some of her characters are offered redemption, in the darker fiction, there is no 'recovery', only an abiding sense of nightmarish uncertainty. Of the more obviously Gothic of her Cornish novels *The King's General*, *Jamaica Inn*, *Rebecca*, and *My Cousin Rachel*, only Mary Yellen finds light and freedom, but this involves leaving Cornwall and turning her face eastward alongside her lover Jim Merlyn. The disabled heroine of *The King's General*, Honor Harris remains in Cornwall but the love of her life is exiled. The ever-unnamed second Mrs De Winter in *Rebecca* is also displaced and filled with a longing for Cornwall so strong it could be equated with the original conception of nostalgia which saw it as literal *homesickness*. In *My Cousin Rachel*, Rachel is destroyed while Philip Ashley remains forever tormented. To a certain extent, these endings go against the popular view of Du Maurier's writing of Cornwall, where the emphasis tends to be on her identification with the beauty and wildness of the countryside. Yet as Horner and Zlosnik put it,

> Cornwall, as constructed by du Maurier, is a landscape imbued with both temptation and danger, as well as delight. [...] Du Maurier's novels, which appear to portray Cornwall positively as a place of freedom, space and authenticity, simultaneously portray that very freedom as dangerous in its evocation of an 'other' self that threatens the main character with psychic fragmentation. (1998, 66–67)

This certainly points to a Romanticised *and* a Gothicised version of the Cornish landscape as well as to authorial identification with the 'strangeness' of the place. There is, however, a distinction in many of the novels which is often missed by scholars: the north coast of Cornwall is the location of wildness including Bodmin Moor, while the south coast is mild, comfortable and easy terrain to navigate, such as the beautiful Frenchman's Creek. And so it is that Mary Yellen speaks of her horror at the difference in terrain when she arrives in the straitened circumstances that have forced her from her home in the South to live at Jamaica Inn located in the North on Bodmin Moor. Thus, there is light and darkness here. And while it may be the romantic construction of Cornwall throughout du Maurier's writing that has had the most lasting legacy on subsequent imaginings of the Cornish landscape, her vision of Cornwall is often far darker than it first appears.

The 'alien' landscape of Cornwall has inspired very many writers; du Maurier was not the first to tap into the dark romance offered by the Cornish countryside. Some of the most illustrious English writers have had a fascination with Cornwall and its ancient landscape littered with stone circles, relics, ancient wells, and the dark chasms of its mines. Wilkie Collins, Bram Stoker, and Arthur Conan Doyle all fell under the Cornish spell. Collins, writing in the 1850s, says that Cornwall is 'still too rarely visited and too little known' (1851, 2). He speaks of 'the grand and varied scenery; the mighty Druid relics; the quaint legends; the deep, dark mines; the venerable remains of early Christianity' (1851, 2–3). At this time, the railway did not reach down into Cornwall, and it was more easily romanticised and imaginable as a Gothic, marginalised space. However, this sense of Cornwall as a land of mist and magic has persisted, in large part due to the legacy of du Maurier. Westland argues that her vision of Cornwall endures because of its imaginative construction: Cornwall as strange fiction. She says,

> For her readers, whatever scarred Cornish scenes may meet our waking eyes in the twenty-first century, we can regain at will those imagined

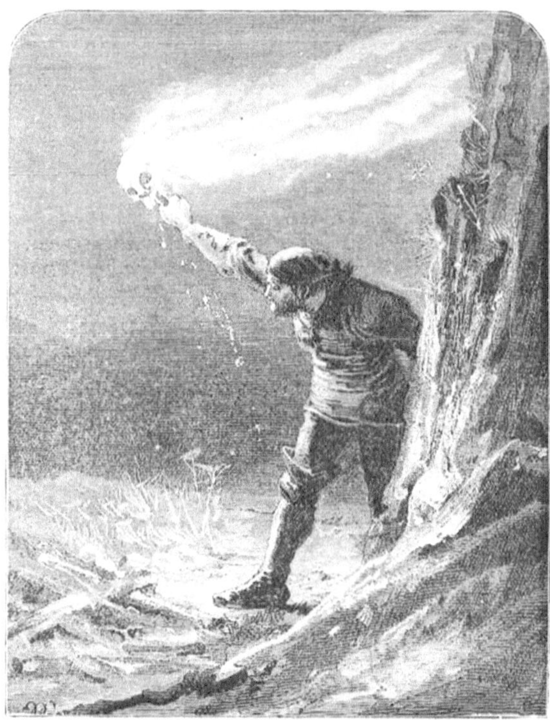

Figure 6 'The Wrecker, "With Flame, as of Streaming Hair"' (engraving), English School, (Nineteenth century) / Private Collection / © Look and Learn / Bridgeman Images.

> domains simply by opening the pages of Daphne du Maurier's novels, and wander her cliffs and creeks with a dreamer's impunity. (2007, 121)

This is Cornwall as an imagined landscape: wild, romantic, untameable, beautiful, and dark. These are the landscapes that encompass the moors of *Jamaica Inn*, the soft air of the Helford river inlets in *Frenchman's Creek* and the mysterious piles of Manderley and Menabilly with their dark secrets, the turbulent seas of *Rebecca* and imagined back through time in *The House on the Strand* and *The King's General*. If, as Robert Mighall asserts, a major feature of the Gothic mode 'is the imputation of anachronism as a source of disorder or fear' (2003, 249), then du Maurier's Cornwall becomes the perfect imaginative fiction of a Gothic site.

Sally Beauman equates history and geography in *My Cousin Rachel* with a sense of disquiet and a sense of dislocation. She says, 'From the first, there is a sense of displacement. We never learn the exact era in which the novel's event's take place, which gives it a curious, dreamlike air of timelessness. And this Cornish estate, unnamed in the novel, has all the fictional allure ruthlessly scraped away' (2007, 173). Indeed, the novel opens with a very unromanticised scene with Ambrose showing his very young cousin Philip the corpse of a murdered man hanging on a gibbet at a crossroads. Ambrose and Philip live on a farming estate on the Cornish coast. They inhabit a patriarchal, homosocial world, free of polite niceties, which seems not to have changed for decades. This comfortable existence is disrupted after Ambrose is forced to travel to Italy for his health. While he is there, he meets, and unexpectedly marries, his half Italian, half Cornish cousin Rachel. During this marriage, Philip, now reached early manhood and running the estate, receives increasingly distressed letters from Ambrose who subsequently dies in Italy. Philip, deeply disturbed and suspicious, is surprised to learn that Rachel is coming to Cornwall to see Ambrose's home. For the rest of the novel, there is a murky mixture of passion, obsession, an attempt at sexual and marital possession, and finally at least one, yet perhaps two murders. Did Rachel poison Ambrose and then attempt to poison Philip? Or did both become violent and paranoid as the result of a hereditary brain tumour? Jess Cox has recently defined the novel as neo-Victorian sensation fiction, discussing it alongside M. E. Braddon's *Lady Audley's Secret* (2019). However, we argue that it can be more closely aligned with Henry James's Gothic novella *The Turn of the Screw*, a text that '*won't* tell, [...] not in any literal vulgar way' (1898, 147). Are there ghosts or are there not? Is the governess mad and bad, or sane and saintly? *My Cousin Rachel* won't tell either. 'Was Rachel innocent or guilty?' (4) is a question that resists answer. Did she poison Ambrose and/or Philip or did she not? In both texts, the refusal of certainty produces a strange doubling of the female characters – both good and evil, sane, and mad at the same time. Their ambiguity also produces a concurrent shadow text where each reading can or may be the spectre of the other, where each text (and the implied reader) is, (as is Philip), 'haunted by doubt' (4). Witches are common in Cornish folklore and practice, but the 'witch' here is Rachel who produces shadows of herself for both Philip and the reader.

Italy, Cornwall, and *My Cousin Rachel*

In the novel, there is also a shadowing of place: Italy echoes Cornwall as both are actively embodied in the elusive character of Rachel. Throughout the novel, there is the pervasive oscillation between belonging and not, where inside and outside seem fused and confused, and twixt the other and the double, a pairing that haunts so much Gothic fiction set in Cornwall. *My Cousin*

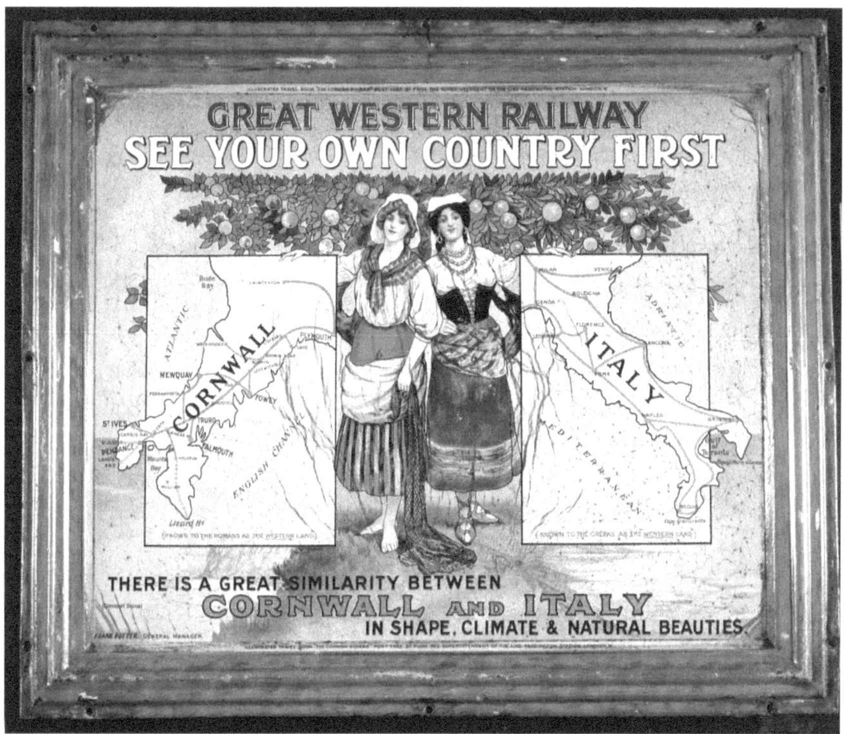

Figure 7 'Cornwall and Italy Great Western Railway Poster'. © NRM/Pictorial Collection/Science & Society Picture Library.

Rachel is a product of the legacy of a Gothic that originally looked elsewhere – to the Continent and, in the first Gothic novel, *The Castle of Otranto*, to Italy. William Hughes argues that '*The Castle of Otranto* [...] quietly aligns the distant corners of contemporary England with the historical south of Italy' (2018, 5). This is a link that du Maurier herself also makes, but she aligns Italy directly with Cornwall. She begins chapter one of her travelogue *Vanishing Cornwall* in this way:

> Cornwall projects from the body of England much as Italy falls from the land mass of central Europe. The two peninsulas, so dis-similar in size, are curiously alike in shape; both long, narrow, terminating in a pincer movement – the claw of Cornwall probing the grey Atlantic, while Italy's high-heeled boot, more delicately formed, treads the Ionian Sea. Resemblance goes further, for each has a river in the north, spanning its breadth and flowing eastward. [...] The analogy might be pushed to its limit, comparing Italy's vertebrae, the central Apennines, with

> Cornwall's backbone, that high hinterland running from north to south. (1967/2012, 9)

Du Maurier does indeed 'push the analogy' and makes the connections (at least in her own mind) clear. These connections are written into *My Cousin Rachel*, where it is Rachel herself who forms the bridge between Italy and Cornwall. And although her father's family are Cornish, still to Philip it seems that at times 'she reeked of old Rome' (92) (famously it has oft been said that during their occupation of England, Romans never made it into Cornwall). In coming to Cornwall, Rachel is transplanted just as are the plants; the camellias and laburnum are relocated from foreign shores to Ambrose's English (Cornish) garden. Rachel says of Ambrose, 'He had a great theory, you know, that I should shrink and shiver in the English climate, especially the damp Cornish one; he called me a green-house plant, fit only for expert cultivation and quite useless in the common soil' (81–82). Ambrose sees his garden as 'a form of creation' (9), but his friends see it as a warped and incorrect type of fertility and 'urge him to settle down into domestic bliss and rear a family instead of rhododendrons' (9). Frankenstein-like, perhaps Ambrose is indulging in the wrong type of creation – a hothouse 'forcing' or unnatural manipulation of the foreign plants into the Cornish landscape. In an echo of both *Rebecca* and *The King's General*, there is infertility here too; Rachel has lost a baby and cannot have another one.

Ambrose declares, 'I shall bring back plants that nobody else has got. We'll see how the demons thrive in Cornish soil' (11). And, at least for a time, they do thrive: 'He brought back heaven knows how many trees, shrubs, flowers, plants of every form and colour. Camellias were his passion. We started a plantation for them alone, and whether he had green fingers or a wizard's touch I do not know, but they flourished from the first' (11). Foreign and yet bedded into Cornish soil; from elsewhere and yet not, these plants are transposed into the 'forcing ground' (88). In the Foreword to *EcoGothic Gardens*, William Hughes considers the Gothic nature of gardens and their cultivation. He states,

> The process and discipline of gardening endows those who police the borders of domestic(ated) space with righteousness as much as with the power and authority to cut and to mutilate, to burn and to poison, to judge and to approve or exclude, on the grounds of colour, of gender or of national origin. (2020, xiv)

Both the plants and Rachel's own status equate to Cornwall's own as being of-England and yet, split by the Tamar and, with a fierce and proud nationalism still present, not of-England. The liminality and indeterminacy of the space of Cornwall are echoed in the (perhaps) misinterpreted and misunderstood character of Rachel. Belonging and not belonging breeds uncertainty, mistrust, and an uncanny feeling of home-and-not-at-home. Yet, in the first flush of infatuation, Ambrose writes to Philip from Italy, 'She is just as English as you or I in her ways and outlook, and might have been living beside the Tamar yesterday' (15).

When Ambrose wrote this, however, Rachel was not living by the Tamar. Indeed, the Florence that is her home is much more central to the Italian landmass than Cornwall is to England. As du Maurier says of Italy and Cornwall, finally perhaps,

> the parallels can be dismissed, the map of Europe folded, and Italy, birthplace of the Roman Empire, cradle of the Renaissance, centre of art and learning throughout the centuries, culminating today in a new brilliance of industrial achievement and design, be left to her immortality. Cornwall, little known, of small significance, remains the tail of England. (2012, 9)

In fact, it is Philip who is living 'out of the world' and who is resident in one of the most remote corners of England. As Rachel tells him later, 'You have not travelled, save the once. You know very little of the world' (296). In the introduction to *Gothic Britain*, commenting on *The Castle of Otranto*, Hughes says,

> The Gothic [...] was from its very origins as much concerned with the culturally temporal as with the literally geographical. In highlighting and addressing the uncanniness of the periphery, it makes commentary upon the power of the centre to comprehend and contain that which it perceives and constructs as Other. The provincial is thus that which is gazed upon by one who has the right to comment on it, rationalise it, render it familiar. (2018, 6)

In *My Cousin Rachel*, however, as in other texts of du Maurier's Cornish Gothic oeuvre, this is complicated and there is ever a slippage between the concept of the 'centre' and that of the 'periphery'. If, both through place (Florence in particular), and character (Rachel and to a lesser extent Rainaldi), the Other and the foreign is identified as Italy, what happens when the view from the 'centre' that places Italy and the Italians as Other, itself originates from the *periphery* of Cornwall? In this scenario, the 'view from the centre' is not central at all. Yet in the novel, Philip's is the central viewpoint, with his fantasy of the absent Ambrose's point of view inflecting and colouring everything he sees about him. (And perhaps it is not too much of a push to point out the echoing of Ambrose's name with that of the fallen and lusting Ambrosio of Lewis' *The Monk* [1796]). Philip ultimately holds the power and comments on and finally condemns the Other in the doomed form of Rachel. Yet perhaps he himself sees aslant: the view of a sheltered and inexperienced boy-man from the very tip of England may not be accurate or properly centred. There is a deep and Gothicised destabilisation of both the male point of view and the conception of the 'centre'; Philip and Ambrose become therefore the hysterics.

Beauman identifies an indivisible rift between Italy and Cornwall. She says,

> Two worlds collide. [...] On the one hand we have England and the Ashley estates, a dour, feudal enclave fiercely resistant to social or political change, a world in which women are marginalised, their influence regarded with a distaste bordering on revulsion. On the other, we have Florence, [...] a place of profligacy, deadly intrigue and sexual sophistication. In England, we find ourselves on a man's estates; in Florence, crucially, we are on female territory. (2007, 174)

Yet beyond this more obvious reading, there is a shift in perception; a layering and (aptly for Cornish heritage) a fundamental undermining of spaces, places, and gender power-plays. And at the centre is Rachel acting as a bridge between Italy and Cornwall. Rachel's passion, as was Ambrose's, is gardens and she decides to build an Italian-esque sunken water garden on Philip's Cornish estate. In the world of Gothic fiction, this is a mistake – a foreign invasion that will not be tolerated. Ambrose was allowed to garden; he could import plants from elsewhere with impunity, if not without some censure from the locals. Rachel's attempt to garden on this Cornish estate — to bring something of Italy into this landscape — is doomed and disastrous. To construct the water garden, a chasm is created which has an ineffective and treacherous bridge hanging over it. As the foreman tells Philip, 'The planking looks firm enough to the eye, but it doesn't bear no weight upon it' (323). It may look solid, but it will inevitably fail. Just as Philip allows Rachel to walk on to the bridge, knowing full well that he is sending her to her death after she refuses his continued offer of marriage, in full possession of himself, he notices, 'She looked much as I had seen her first, ten months ago, except that it was summer. The scent of the new cut grass was in the air. A butterfly flew past in happy flight. The pigeons cooed from the great trees beyond the lawn' (330). After the turbulence and the storms, things are now quiet, and we are firmly in Cornwall. This is a domestic, pastoral idyll that will endure. It is the flimsy bridge that will crack and fail, taking the independent Rachel with it. Finally, after a pause, Philip goes to find her: 'Part of the bridge still remained and hung suspended, grotesque and horrible, like a swinging ladder'

(335), or like the swinging gibbet where the book began with the corpse of the executed man who 'swung between the earth and the sky upon his gibbet, or, as my cousin Ambrose told me, betwixt heaven and hell' (1). As Philip reflects later, this swinging corpse of the wife-murderer could be 'my own shadow' (7). In his lust and attempt to control Rachel, it is he who can be said to echo Ambrosio of *The Monk* and not his cousin Ambrose.

Land of Mist and Magic

Alongside the darker tropes, du Maurier's novels are filled with adventure, mystery, romance, and hints of the supernatural. The Cornish landscape becomes a dramatic persona in her work, a vital and active component rather than a simple setting. Inextricably linked to the sometimes wild and always changeable weather, the landscapes exude an atmosphere of a different sort, one that is sometimes magical and sometimes terrible. In du Maurier's work, the descriptions of Cornwall spring off the page alive; keyed into conceptions of the sublime, the pastoral and the Gothic, the landscape becomes shrouded in secretive mystery and enigma. This sense of the Cornish landscape as remote, hidden, possessive, and mysterious, pervades du Maurier's work and provides one of the lasting legacies that are called on by touristic and fictional imaginings of Cornwall. This is a magical place unlike anywhere else – a space where the landscape itself is strange, animated, and alive in its ungraspable otherness.

At the crux of the narrative of *My Cousin Rachel*, the time around Philip's birthday, the weather and the landscape come to the fore. In an ecstasy of love, adoration, and infatuation, Philip decides to legally bequeath his whole estate and all his wealth to Rachel at the very chiming of his twenty-fifth birthday, the date when he inherits Ambrose's estate. During this time, the landscape folds itself around him, echoing his feelings of sublime enchantment. After he has signed the documents that will gift everything to Rachel, he rides home: 'The sun was sinking beyond the westward bay, flaming the quiet sky, darkening the water, and the rounded face of the near full moon showed plain over the eastern hills' (246). This is the Cornish landscape in all its sublime beauty, but there is a threat here too. The sky is flaming, the water darkening, and the moon is not yet full: there is more to come. Still, around this time, Philip is immersed in a fairytale landscape:

> The park, as I entered it, had all the grace of fairy tale, even the cattle, plodding down to drink at their trough beside the pool, were creatures of enchantment, lending themselves to beauty. The jackdaws were building high, they flapped and straddled their untidy nests in the tall

> trees near to the avenue, and from the house and the stables I could see the blue smoke curling from the chimneys […]. All this was old to me, long-known and loved, possessed from babyhood; yet now it held new magic. (247)

Philip is seeing with new eyes, but what he sees is not necessarily 'true', it is a 'fairy tale', an 'enchantment' that holds 'new magic'. This landscape is not the stolid, materialistic, legalistic, inherited lands and the house which, before too long, it becomes. It is, in short, a fantasy, or (if we delve back into some of the older feminisms), a phallocentric phantasy.

This of course echoes what Rachel says about how Ambrose felt about her. She tells Philip that after Ambrose fell in love with her, 'He was like someone sleeping who woke suddenly and found the world', she says 'Ambrose had woken to me just as some men wake to religion. He became obsessed in the same fashion […]. Finding me was ecstasy to him for one brief moment, and then came catastrophe' (103–4). Philip and Ambrose are doubled throughout the novel; however, if Rachel is 'two persons' (320), then perhaps Philip is right, and he and Ambrose are one. This doubling of Philip and Ambrose is discussed by Beauman (2007) and Horner and Zlosnik (1998). At the beginning of the novel when Philip retrospectively reflects, after Rachel's death, on his affinity with Ambrose, he says, 'I have become so like him that I might be his ghost. My eyes are his eyes, my features his features. […] I have wondered lately if, when he died, […] whether his spirit left his body and came home here to mine' (4–5). But which home? The real one or the fantasy? Ambrose haunts Philip. Just before he gives (quite literally) everything to Rachel, Philip goes for a swim:

> The moonlight made a ghostly path for me, and the shadows, eerie and fantastic, lurked behind the trees. Where my path divided into two, one taking me to the cedar walk and the other to the new terrace above, I heard a rustle where the trees grew thickest, and suddenly to my nostrils came that rank vixen smell about me in the air, tainting the very leaves under my feet. (250)

Two paths, two Rachels, and a doubling of Philip/Ambrose. And beware, one path will taint and corrupt – a ghost path that sheds the scent of hidden, bestial, femaleness.

This trope of doubling, and the boundary-dissolving hysteria it implies, is, of course, a staple of Gothic literature. *My Cousin Rachel* is a fictive autobiography. As Coral Howells says:

> Such narratives [i.e. autobiographies] are themselves labyrinthine structures, endlessly doubling between real life stories and fictional reconstructions. These features produce uncanny effects, for ghost figures the secret life of memory while split selves and dark doubles provide images for psychic repression and self-alienation. [...] That blurring of boundaries between the real and the imaginary would account for a fascination with transgression as these narrators negotiate border crossings between dreams and waking, truth and lies, even between life and death. (2007, 108)

This doubling blurs distinctions between fantasy and reality. The inner world Philip inhabits and the actual Cornish landscape, sleeping, waking, truth, fiction, become indecipherable and indivisible. Rachel Mosely looks at the romanticised construction of Cornwall saying, 'Cornish folklore, as well as literature set in the county, often features hauntings and magical creatures, and the significance of the past in the present is ever-present in the Cornish landscape, in the form of granite tors, standing stones and the ruins of Cornwall's tin and copper mining industrial history' (2013, 646). This again is an animated landscape: the Cornish landscape is not passive, it is active, imbued with traces of the past – it is alive and sentient.

This blurring of the material world and that of the fantastic, which confuse distinctions between choice and fate, becomes embodied in the mass of the granite stone that Ambrose erected:

> It was our highest point of land, saving the beacon to the south, and had a fine view over the woods and the valley to the open sea. The trees fringing the path, planted by Ambrose and his father before him, gave shelter. [...] At the end of the path, topping the woods, before plunging to descent and the keeper's cottage in the gully, Ambrose had set up a piece of granite. "This,' he said to me, half joking, half in earnest, 'can serve me for tombstone when I die'. (203–4)

This granite slab is an anomaly. Cornwall is littered with standing stones; great slabs of granite that have probably stood for thousands of years and which we like to think signify ancient rituals, burial sites, and forgotten religious practices. Du Maurier could have chosen the granite slab to be one of these stones that dot the Cornish terrain. And yet it was Ambrose who placed this phallic stone, and eventually, in Philip's fevered imagination, it is this monument that forces the chasm between him and Rachel: 'I knew [...] what had come between Rachel and myself. The granite slab, above the valley in the woods' (278).

During the stilted and awkward walk with Rachel on his birthday after he has given her everything, they accidentally come across it:

> suddenly we were upon the granite stone above the valley, which I had forgotten awaited us at the termination of the path. I turned swiftly into the trees, so as to avoid it, but too late. She had already seen it, dark and square among the trees, and letting go my hand stood still and stared at it.
>
> [...] She made no comment on the monument, nor did I, but somehow that great slab of granite was with us as we walked. [...] I thought to myself [...] the slab of granite will be a barrier between us, and will grow in magnitude. [...]
>
> What demon took us to that granite stone, what lapse of memory? [...] The slab of granite, tall and proud, would have taken on the substance of the man himself, whom, through fault of circumstance, she had not permitted to return to die at home, but who lay many hundred miles away, in the Protestant cemetery in Florence. (263–64)

Philip has taken the wrong path. And, for all that it is a relatively newly erected stone, it carries significance beyond itself. Cornwall sits mainly on granite. It is the hard, ungiving substance that underlies the beauty of both the tame and the wild Cornish countryside. Cornwall is a mined county, littered with deep antique shafts as well as prehistoric burial mounds and caves. The underneath or underside of Cornwall is important in all depictions of Cornwall, but most particularly in the Gothic. As Ruth Heholt has written elsewhere, 'there are exotic depths to Cornwall: something seeps through the granite' (2018, 207). Ambrose erected the stone, and Philip has buried his letter that damns Rachel in Ambrose's hand beneath it. Philip becomes desperate to 'forget the granite slab and what it stood for in our inner selves. Last night I had walked to the beacon head under the full moon, in exultation, sleep-walking, in a dream. To-night, though in the intervening hours I had woken to the wealth of the whole world, I had woken to shadows too' (265–66). Philip has indeed woken up (or is at least in the process of doing so). The dreams will pass and the shadows will remain, as the granite that Ambrose erected embeds itself into the Cornish landscape; a phallocentric erection that obtrudes from the earth. Something of Ambrose's that will indeed stand between Philip and Rachel.

Adaptations and Afterlives

Du Maurier's Cornwall extends beyond the boundaries of the granite peninsular itself. Stretching out from the place/time of her Cornish works, her imagined Cornwall leaves a strong legacy. In part at least, because of their setting, her novels lend themselves to cinematic and televisual adaptation. These include a surprising 1952 adaptation of *My Cousin Rachel* (starring Richard Burton and Olivia de Haviland) and a newer adaptation in 2017, directed by Roger Michell. In this latter film, sea, rocks, and coast are vitally important, to the extent that in this adaptation, rather than falling from a bridge over an Italian garden, Rachel dies by riding on an unstable cliff path which collapses, sending her plunging to her death. Rachel is ignorant of local knowledge while Phillip knows it well having nearly befallen its treachery earlier on in the film. Rachel Mosely usefully takes a whole article to examine the imagery of women on cliffs in Cornwall. She claims that there is a key 'place-image' of Cornwall, 'the woman on the cliff top, at the edge' (2013, 644). Mosely says the cliff edge is 'a space of reflection about possibility, identity and belonging' (2013, p. 656). However, if this is so, it is a location that fails Rachel in the film. Mosely also posits the cliff edge as a site of transgression and even sexuality, which is perhaps why the (unacceptably) sexually mature Rachel literally goes over the edge. Yet despite the fact that the landscape 'does for' Rachel in a way that is more direct than in the novel, this adaptation strips out many of the telling indicators of space, place, and the Gothic that permeate the book. The corpse hanging at the crossroads on the gibbet is lost, thereby weakening the link between Philip and the wife-killer; let off the hook we might say. The phallic granite stone that fuses Ambrose and Philip, does not appear, and most notably, Cornwall itself is stripped out of the narrative.

In the commentary on the DVD, director Roger Michell says, 'I made a choice not to try and either shoot this film in Cornwall or even actually to set the film in Cornwall. […] I didn't want it to cross-over into a kind of Poldark world. […] I thought that may be confusing or unhelpful. So this is set in a sort of vague West Country, Dorset-y, Wessex-y sort of Hardy-esque world' (Michell, 2017). And why is this? Michell cites 'Poldark world', another imagining of Cornwall. Yet he has taken this as a 'reality' of Cornwall (at least he posits it as such in the public imagination), whereas, of course, it is just another fiction. Michell seems to have lost the fact that (at least sometimes) Cornwall is a real place and that very many of the audience coming to see a du Maurier adaptation will assume a Cornish setting anyway, making their own romance out of its very present absence. Michell filmed in Devon but refuses to name any location. Cornwall is (at least from his point of view) erased, becoming absent and lacking in any real-world signifier that might tether it either to reality or to the mainland. Ironically, Michell's erasure places Cornwall back into the Gothic.

Legacies of du Maurier's Gothic Cornwall are everywhere and one of the most potent imaginings of a magical and mystical Kernow come with the tourist construction of the place. At the time of writing, the most recent imagining of Cornwall as a dark, sometimes destructive place, is the award-winning indie film *Bait.* Written and directed by Mark Jenkin *Bait* is a tale of two imagined worlds of Cornwall colliding: the traditional fishing village where life is a struggle and hardship is an everyday reality, and the tourist, second-homer version of the same village and way of life. The story documents the clash between the one-time fishermen Martin and Steven Ward and the incoming tourists from London who have purchased their family's cottage and turned it into a B&B. As the son of the Cornish man and the daughter from London form a romantic liaison, tensions boil over and end in tragedy. *Bait* is filled with hints of uncanny and the supernatural. There are impossibilities that flash through some scenes – people where they can't possibly be, prophetic flashes forward to the violence that is to come, ghosts lurking on the periphery, including one that helpfully tells Martin where to put his lobster pots. Jessica Kiang cites the 'Nic Roeg-ian use of flashforward edits that create a doomy sense of déjà vu as the film twists towards tragedy' (2019, 7). Director Nic Roeg is mentioned quite often in relation to *Bait.* In an interesting aside, Roeg directed the film adaptation of du Maurier's story 'Don't Look Now' which Mark Jenkin refers to in the film commentary. 'Don't Look Now' is set in Italy. In *Bait*, there is an overriding and unrelenting sense of tension and unease that echoes with *My Cousin Rachel*: something *is* going to go wrong. Ian Mantgani in *Sight and Sound* talks about 'the film's salty, queasy sense of suspicion, outrage and doom'. Likening it to *The Wicker Man* and *Straw Dogs*, he says it uses the 'English wyrd and outsider intrusion' (2019). Yet, while critics such as Mantgani and Stephen Dalton align *Bait* with the folk horror tradition, (which we examine in Chapter 3), in an article on *The Medium* website, Dan E. Smith says firmly, '*Bait* understands the Gothic' (2019). The whole aesthetic of the film, with its scratches and imperfections, the shadows thrown by the noirish high contrast monochrome, the claustrophobia of the village contrasted with the magnificent seascapes, speaks to a space where light is unlikely to penetrate for long. The aesthetic also harks back to the past, and in proper Gothic traditions, *The Skinny* film magazine notes that 'it's like a print from the early days of cinema that's been rescued from some sloppy archivist's dank shed or dusty loft'. It is, the article says, as if 'it's some found object from the silent era' (Dunn, 2019); this may be overstated, but reference to both John Grierson's 'principles of documentary' (i.e. observations of life, don't use actors) and his documentary *Granton Trawler* made in 1934 focused on fishermen and shot in black and white, is very much apparent.

Bait presents Cornwall as strange fiction, mixing a documentary style with that of weird fiction. It offers two differing imaginings of Cornwall – the traditional view where livelihood depends on the environment versus the wealthy 'outsider' version of the landscape – and the disparity between these ideas of Cornwall leads inevitably to violence. The landscapes in *Bait* swing from the romantically sublime to an anti-pastoral realism. The seascapes are gorgeous, but the tiny village is enclosed and overrun, and apart from on the seaward side, there is no sense of any space beyond the houses. The village becomes the whole world, with the sea representing the only way out and the only clear line of sight. In this vision of Cornwall, it is London that is absent/imagined, occupying a margin we cannot see. Robert Mighall says starkly, 'The "Gothic" by definition, is about history and geography' (2003, xiv), and so is *Bait*. The 'real' past (fishing) is being lost even as it is being commodified as a tourist novelty and spectacle. The Londoners deck out the ex-fisherman's cottage they have bought with pseudo-fishing industry paraphernalia – nets and a false porthole, an anchor door knocker. This is a re-imagining of a past that isn't quite gone yet, but which is in deep decline, and this produces a disconcerting sense of a wrong sort of mirroring or echoing. The fishermen are still 'there', but the tourist imagining of their way of life is drowning out and superseding the real. Mighall claims that 'the Gothic carries a (pseudo-) historical inflection' (2003, xv), and this is apparent in *Bait*, but the past is too close and not quite done with. Talking about *The Castle of Otranto*, William Hughes says it is presented 'as an artefact whose implications are relevant to more than one historical period, and whose cultural status draws upon the perception of localised and distant geographies' (2018, 2). As with *My Cousin Rachel* and much regional Gothic which presents the view from the periphery, *Bait* skews the idea of what is 'localised' and what 'distant'. There is a doubling of both time and space in the film that comes from the two competing imaginings of Cornwall and what it means. Hughes claims that for the Gothic,

> the conflict between metropolitan and regional identities is historically as fundamental to the structure of the genre as the opposition of past to present [...]. Gothic, in other words, arguably embodies a consistent but often understated commitment to the troubled coexistence of the regional and the metropolitan, to both margin and centre as a tense arena. (2018, 15)

In *Bait*, there is complete confusion over what is past and what is present, what is real and what is imagined. The incomers impose a centrist/tourist romanticised re-creation of the past and the present, bringing *in* a version of Cornwall and its industrial past that threatens to obliterate both. Following postmodern aesthetics of simulation, the imagined 'unreal' becomes more real than 'reality'; the tourist version of place and history may well overwrite both the past and the fishing, yet the way of life (somehow) continues to hang on. That simulation is by nature uncanny. The fishing net decorations are not real, the doorknob is not an anchor; there is a ghost in the fake porthole. The Londoners have brought their romanticised version of Cornwall (and they have bought it in). In the commentary to *Bait*, Mark Kermode in conversation with Mark Jenkin says 'they've been told something that isn't there. [...] Everyone's living in a place they've been told a different version of' (2019). The tourist view of Cornwall is always inflected by du Maurier's work, but as we saw with *My Cousin Rachel*, despite (because of?) this selling of 'du Maurier country', Cornwall can be a very dark place. Jenkin says of the co-existence of fishing and tourism, 'the story has quickly become one of haves and have-nots. Not a black-and-white story but one pulsing away within the grey areas. Just below the surface of the wild Atlantic, resting in the "quaint" harbour' (BFI Commentary book). In *Bait*, it is the attempted relationship between the 'insider' Cornish young man Neil Ward and the 'outsider' daughter of the second homeowners that leads to Neil's death. Another fragile bridge is undermined, and someone dies because of a failed union of the inside and the outside. Fred Botting and Justin D. Edwards, talking about Capitalist inter- and transnationalism say that the inevitable decentring associated with these market flows 'turns modern ways of thinking, believing, being and narrating inside-out and upside-down, generating a new sense of anxiety about borders, identities and futures' (2013, 13). In du Maurier's work and in Jenkin's *Bait*, ideas of possession, ownership, and property, lead to a slippage between the sense of inside and out, the 'home' and the 'foreign', belonging and not. In these strange fictions set in the periphery, Cornwall may be imagined, but Kernow becomes a very dark Gothic space.

CHAPTER 2

SUPERSENSORY GOTHIC KERNOW: *MAGIC, MYSTICISM,* AND *THE ESOTERIC AESTHETICS* OF *EMERGENCE*

This chapter focuses on the output of artists who have worked with elements of the Cornish landscape, its geology, and its prehistoric monuments as a means of engaging with magic and mysticism. Such engagements are however rarely considered through the lens of the Gothic. Often, and instead, this type of work is seen in the terms of neo-pagan culture, Celtic studies, neo-romanticism, or, more simply, as fine art or poetry. However, as we show, if we regard this body of work in relation to Gothic tropes, concerns, and modalities, we can gain a better grasp of the wide scope of Gothic's reach into all kinds of fields of creative activity, and not just within popular fiction.

Gothic studies concepts of otherness, animism, and the sublime provide the theoretical foundation for the chapter's critical engagement with such work. Reference to these terms will help us to map the affiliations of such work to the peculiar nature of the Cornish Gothic. In addition, our focus will fall not just on the artistic end-product as text or artefact but also on the methods and contexts that are employed to produce them. These methods are integral to the cross-over between magical and artistic practice. We will therefore pay specific attention to an artistic working practice that we will call an 'aesthetics of emergence'. We argue that such emergent practice can itself be usefully claimed for Gothic with the technique used by many of the visual artists referred to in this chapter. As the chapter goes on to explore, emergent practice is often used to generate a strong imaginative and phantasmagorical communication with the specifics of place. It is employed often as a method of engagement with the occult (as in divining that which is hidden, obscure, or not perceptible with the usual senses), and is used as a means of embracing the creative power of the irrational and the happenstance. As such, the chapter seeks to demonstrate that both automatism, as an artistic technique, and animism carry with them a special relationship with Gothic and that they are integral to a characteristic creative engagement with the Cornish landscape and its mythos.

Ithell Colquhoun's Psychomorphological Cornish Mysteries

The principal focus of the chapter is the work of artist and magician, Ithell Colquhoun (1906–1988). We will go on to discuss the work of other artists later in the chapter in terms of the legacy of her work, her methods, and her Gothic relationship with the stuff of Cornwall. A painter, poet, writer, and practising occultist, Colquhoun lived in Cornwall for 40 years (Hale, 2020, 6). Much like du Maurier, she regarded Cornwall as a place of creative escape and contemplative quietude: 'after years of the blitz I felt that here I could find some humble refuge from the claustrophobic fright of cities' (Colquhoun, 2016, 21). Her writing and visual practice provide an enriching comparison to du Maurier's more sensationalist romantic vision of the region. While different in nature, both develop their creative identity through a libidinal, erotic relationship with land and sea. Cornwall stands as a productive and generative 'Other' in their creative landscape. As Gemma Gary says, 'Colquhoun's adopted landscape, in which she sought out and immersed herself in the liminal, the transformative, and the numinous, was the West of Cornwall' (Gary, 2019). With a long-standing interest in the occult arts, including alchemy, and operating within the milieu of surrealism, Colquhoun uses various media in what is best described as a series of subtle workings. These are often focused on flows and energies and are part of an imaginative vision where all things are connected through webs of correspondences and suggestions. Unlike du Maurier, the body of Colquhoun's work must therefore be regarded as Gothic in non-generic and atypical terms. As with J. M. W. Turner, whose paintings of Cornwall use rock, sea, and light to shrink down the agentic sphere of the human, Colquhoun's landscape imagery is not focused simply on observational representation. Instead, it seeks out something that lies far beyond representation and it is in that quest, which is for her an occult practice as well as for others practising in that same sphere, that the route to the Gothic can be found.

Even though her novella *The Goose of Hermogenes* (1961) has been categorised as a *roman noir*, to date, Colquhoun's work has not been appraised in terms of its relation to the Gothic. There is however increasing art historical interest in her practice. This is partly down to the hard graft of advocate scholars dedicated to bringing Colquhoun's work to wider attention. These include Richard Shillitoe's analytic and archival book *Ithell Colquhoun: Magician Born of Nature* (2009) and a more recent collection of her writing, *Medea's Charms: Selected Shorter Writings* (2019) alongside his groundbreaking archival website that tracks Colquhoun's visual artwork; Steve Nicholl's edited collection,

The Magical Writings of Ithell Colquhoun (2007) with a focus on her engagement with the magical systems; Eric Ratcliffe's critical appraisal *Ithell Colquhoun: Pioneer, Surrealist, Artist, Occultist, Poet and Author* (2007/2016); Amy Hale's careful scholarship on Colquhoun's magic and art practice, including her book *Ithell Colquhoun: Genius of the Fern Loved Gully* (2020). Colquhoun produced an incredible amount of work throughout her life, leaving her remaining artwork to the National Trust, which is now in the keeping of the Tate in the United Kingdom. Our intention in this chapter is to draw on the material of these scholarly advocates, and on a small, indicative number of Colquhoun's works. This will serve our goal of locating Colquhoun as a foundational figure of the Cornish Gothic, equal to du Maurier although not as widely known. We will also show that Colquhoun too has a lasting and potent legacy. Our focus on her art also serves a secondary purpose to demonstrate the connections between Surrealism and the Gothic, another overlooked area for study. Close consideration of three of her better-known paintings – *Scylla* 1938; *The Sunset Birth* 1942; *The Dance of the Nine Opals* 1942 – alongside poems and other writings, including her short novel *The Goose of Hermogenes* (published in 1961), will help support us in our quest to understand her work as Gothic and its role in establishing lasting patterns in Cornish Gothic.

It should be noted that our approach here is not simply textual: it is important that the methods employed in the mode and context of practice are considered if we are (a) to investigate Colquhoun's work as Gothic, (b) to locate Cornwall's role as catalyst to the creative imagination, and, (c) to challenge and broaden out more convention-based definitions of Gothic to accommodate both fine art practice and, what Genesis P. Orridge named, 'Occulture'.

'Mysterium tremendum et fascinans': Animism and the 'Living Stones' of the Cornish landscape

In *The Living Stones* (first published in 1957), Colquhoun wrote a book-length 'travelogue' account of her move to Lamorna, a village located near the far tip of Cornwall. She writes of being 'overcome by its leafy, water-loud charm' (2016, 20) and it becomes clear that Cornwall has latched on to the deep affinity for the natural world that she developed as a child (Hale 2012, 308). Her engagement with nature is evident in her early still-life paintings of plants, such as *Canna* (1936), where the curves and plush qualities of stems and leaves create a strong sense of movement and vitality, in their soft blue-green hues and kinetic attitude appearing as if underwater. These lush plant forms push beyond the representational and the material used to produce them into realms sensuous, elemental, and imaginary. The evocation of these realms becomes the vital conditions for the way she breathes spirit into representational forms: she confides with her reader 'an animist is what I am' (2016, 20). This short line provides a key to unlocking the magical nature of her romance with Cornwall as well as the enigmatic visual vocabulary and personalised mythos of her art practice. In her embrace of animism, she forges a pathway that later leads to Earth Mysteries, a 'movement' documented so well by Rupert White (2017) in relation to Cornwall. While animism can be described as a nascent property of landscape painting, Colquhoun suffused approach consolidates animism as integral to a broader understanding of Cornwall as a place set apart, a bulwark against spiritual impoverishment.

What is animism? Katherine Swancutt summarises the anthropological definition of animism, as 'both a concept and a way of relating to the world [...] an "animistic" sensibility attributes sentience – or the quality of being "animated" – to a wide range of beings in the world, such as the environment, other persons, animals, plants, spirits, and forces of nature like the ocean, winds, sun, or moon.' (Swancutt, Katherine. 2019. Animism. doi:http:doi.org10.2916419anim. Accessed 12112020.) While other cultures may not regard the otherness of animism as an imaginary, spiritual, and enriching mode of engagement with the world, it certainly is for Colquhoun and other artists working under the glimmering light of a Romantic star. The animistic qualities of her artistic sensibility, and the magical and occult principles that underlie it, where the human body, the land, and the cosmos are all connected, are therefore integral to understanding her work as a subtle and non-generic form of Gothic.

A most vivid articulation of her animistic approach is exemplified in many of Colquhoun's paintings and within her representational aims. A task of the subtle painter is to make the unseen – yet intuited – visible, while making spirits manifest is, of course, the task of the magician and mediums. Colquhoun is both. *Landscape with Antiquities* (painted in 1955) presents us with a two-dimensional, portrait-oriented, aerial map. A white line, betokening a road snakes its way from top to bottom. It is edged with trees or perhaps Cornish hedges (hybrids made of stone, earth, and plants). Smaller lines, some grey, sprout from the leading line, forming three main segments reminiscent of fields. Some are dark red and others green, while the base segment is ochre, yellow-brown. Mainly positioned along the main north–south line/road are various monuments – standing stones, a stone cross, obelisks, barrow; varied tones lend them three-dimensional form and are far larger in scale than the other cartographic features. The composition is carefully balanced, underpinned by the scheme of complementary colours.

Most of the painting's monuments line up diagonally across the upper square of the image while the segments in the lower right triangle of the lower

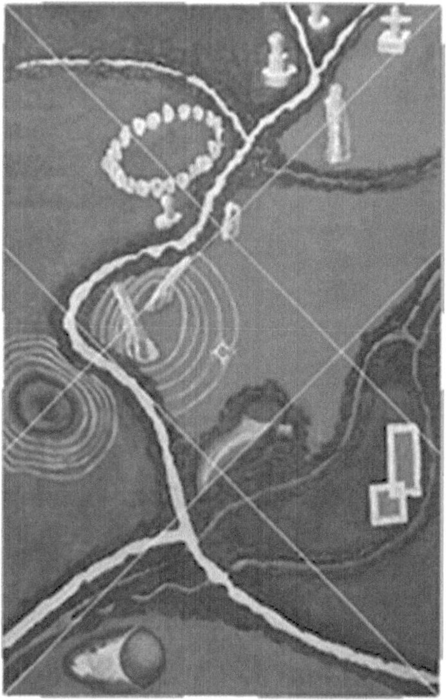

Figure 8 *Landscape with Antiquities* by Ithell Colquhoun (1955). Permission Tate Gallery.

Note: we have overlaid a compositional grid over this painting to demonstrate its compositional scheme.

square are darker tonally than the rest of the image (see Figure 8 with our overlaid grid). In many of Colquhoun's paintings and drawings, concentric circles appear, used as in Celtic art, to connote pulsing energy. Here they are drawn around the two phallic standing stones and again around another feature presented as a red area with a dark interior. These two circles balance one another compositionally and optically in terms of colour complements. These are not however simply used to create graphical interest nor to indicate cartographically the contours of a hill; their purpose is animistic, used to indicate otherwise hidden energetic centres of power and to connect the sexual body to land. Colquhoun argued that Celtic people were more in tune with energetic centres and often marked them with monuments. This conception overlaps with that of leylines, first developed by Alfred Watkins in the early 1920s and later becomes important within post-1960s Earth Mysteries literature (White, 2017).

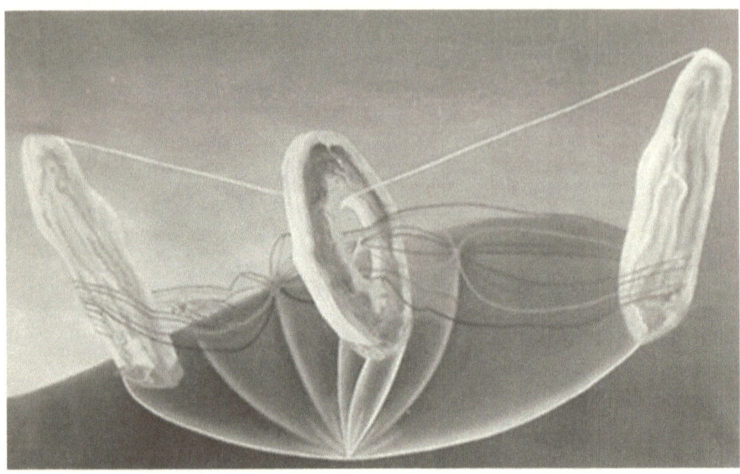

Figure 9 *Sunset Birth* by Ithell Colquhoun (1942). Oil on Canvas. 15.5 x 28 inches. Private Collection.

Ratios and proportions are carefully deployed in the painting, a common feature of Colquhoun's work (Hale 2012, 316). In her hands, these are magical tools, divine principles. Used in conjunction with iconographic elements, an animistic and occult cartography of the landscape is produced in the painting: sacred geometry united with the subtle earth energies of geomancy, revealing a hidden and othered order of the universe. These techniques conjoin to signify that the Cornish landscape is alive, sentient, a conception laden with Gothic mystery: 'Stones that whisper, stones that dance, that play on pipe or fiddle, that tremble at cockcrow, that eat and drink, stones that march as an army – these unhewn slabs of granite hold the secret of the country's inner life' (2016, 64).

The use of concentric circles to depict unseen energies also features within *Sunset Birth* (1942) (Figure 9) and is seen in a more sculptural, contour-defining, and embodied sense in rock-legs of her painting *Scylla* (1938). *Sunset Birth* features a standing stone formation known as Mên-an-Tol ('stone with a hole'), located in the moorland of West Cornwall between St Ives and St Just. A large circular stone with a hole inside measuring around 1.3 metres across is positioned between two upright standing stones. A watercolour, a figurative pencil sketch, and an oil painting exist based on the monument, showing that Colquhoun was experimenting with different colours and forms. In a pencil sketch, a figure of an outstretched, naked woman lies across and through the monument – perhaps as means of connecting and conjuring stone into flesh, a theme that also abides with the women encased in stones in the watercolour

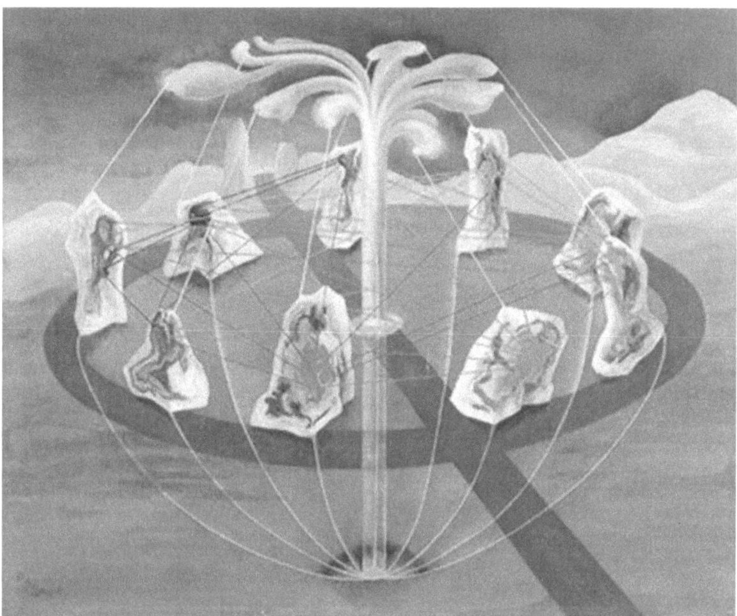

Figure 10 *Dance of the Nine Opals* by Ithell Colquhoun (1942). Oil on Canvas. 22.5 x 28 inches. Permission Tate Gallery.

sketches that seem preliminary to the more resolved *Dance of the Nine Opals* (Figure 10). *Sunset Birth* seems to embody the divine feminine. The figure is magically connected to the monument passing through the central stone's physical and symbolic hole, in an image that alludes to a tradition of fertility or healing rituals at the site. Colquhoun writes of a visit to the monument, she 'crawled from east to west through the ring-like stone [...] as cure for rheumatism and was disappointed with the result, not knowing that in order to be effective the rite should be performed in a state of nudity' (2016, 62).

The female figure of *Sunset Birth* is abstracted, delineated as a series of concentric lines, each of different colours, that follow the length of the body. The lines vibrate optically in accord with the different energies of the subtle body. These are the channels that connect the body's chakras (centres of energy) in Yogic and Tantric traditions to the universe. As a member of the Theosophical Society, Colquhoun was well-versed in such ideas, albeit reinterpreted within the terms of western esotericism. The emphasis on subtle energies is also inherent in the use of colour used as a magical tool as well as a visual device, an approach found throughout Colquhoun's work. In another watercolour painting of the same monument, the round stone pulses with bright pink, clear orange, and deep blue – each bleeding into the other yet also distinct. Translated into pigment and water, she reveals the stones' high spiritual vibration which plays against the visible material substance of hard grey granite. In this, Colquhoun animates the stones bringing them to magical life. By contrast, the oil painting (Figure 10) is less airy than the watercolour: there is burnished and blended consistency to the paint application and the interplay of colours, an approach that echoes Salvador Dali's pristine landscapes. Moving right to left across the painting's background an orange glow conjoins incrementally with its complement, blue. Coming up from the East, this is where day meets night. Colquhoun often seeks to bring opposites together, optically and thematically, weaving an animistic spell from the elemental materiality of pigment and paint mediums. Orange meets blue, bright against the darker hues of the background, translucence meets the opaque to create optical, spectral, and magical vivacity. These elements are orchestrated to produce form and meaning. The painting pivots around a see-sawing lotus flower. This point of conjunction connects and balances stone and body, natural rhythms, and a hidden, othered order beneath the skins of earth and body.

A similar connecting device underlies the eponymous dancers of *Dance of the Nine Opals*, a painting that references the Nine Maidens stone circle that is located not far from Mên-an-Tol. Here, however, the diagrammatic flower is more symmetrically placed, in keeping with the symmetry found in the rest of the painting. Coming from one point of origin, the curved lines resemble that of the segments of a halved orange, helping to describe how the figures on the surface plane sit in three-dimensional space. Additional straight lines create a network above the plane of the green circle, creating connections across the nine stones/figures and to the head of the stylised 'tree' – perhaps the world ash tree Yggdrasil, or, a crown, a Kabbalistic figuration of Kether, and/or, a maypole, around which the figures dance. The lines imply movement, rotation. An opaque diagonal green line, laid against a red, translucent ground, forms the surface of a circle's horizontal plane; the green line suggests entry or exit points, while two literal standing stones form a gateway. This construction balances linear movement and rotation, while linear perspective fleshes three dimensions out a two-dimensional form. Colours, composition, figurative and abstract, energy and form, stone and body, substance and spirit. The balanced play of opposites such as these gives a clue as to what governs the whole artifice. The elements add up to the sophisticated representational animism that in Colquhoun's generative hands becomes a fully fledged symbolic language grounded in the Cornish landscape.

Colquhoun's animism exceeds that found in the genre-based Gothic. It may not seem to be the type of 'return of the repressed' approach typical of folk horror traditions, yet there is certainly a connection with it and we can see it as a form of eco-feminist Gothic that we'll see later on when we discuss ritual and sea witches in more straightforwardly defined Gothic fiction. Colquhoun's Gothic is grounded in a sense of the numinous and esoteric, '*Mysterium tremendum et fascinans*' (fearful and fascinating mystery). Colquhoun's animism is not therefore simple anthropomorphism; it generates instead that rare beast, the mystical Gothic, and demonstrates the vertiginous complexity of an imagination fully open to the stars and generative forces. This Gothic unhinges the anthropocentric, the centred, and the quotidian in a way that cannot be dismissed as a cheap sensational thrill. As Artaud puts it, the surrealist sensibility that Colquhoun embodies sought to bring form to the 'Non-manifested…it is looking beyond forms for the occult and magical presence of a fascinating unreality' (cited Lepetit 2012, 39). Such occult work is therefore doubly determined as Gothic in process, as well as in content. All creative output might be said to be inherently phantasmagorical – yet some sets out in a different direction than that destined for commercial consumption. And, as Hale notes, much of Colquhoun's work was 'experimental' rather than commercial (Hale, 2012, 315).

There is a doubled process at work in Colquhoun's animism: making the unseen, yet intuited, visible is the task of the painter, while making spirits manifest is, of course, the active task of the magician (as opposed to the passive task of the medium). In both, there is an inherent animism that far exceeds the anthropological definition. As part of her compelling strange-making practice, Colquhoun works her esoteric and distinctly female-oriented conception of uncanny into the very strata of the Cornish landscape and, like du Maurier, the Kernow of her imagination. In pursuit of this generative uncanny, she used a range of automatic methods to bring the extrinsic and the spirit world into her work.

Drawing Out the Other: Emergence and Automatism as Gothic Method

Many artists work hard to develop their skills of graphical application, observation, and composition. The honorific term, 'old master' is telling in this regard. It denotes exemplary use and application of materials in terms of precision and construction. Some artists have, however, sought to bring to their practice something of the Other: losing their grip to open up to the vicissitudes of hazard (as in uncertainty and chance) and emergence. British artist, Austin Osman Spare (1886–1956) possessed from an early age an exquisite mastery of line and tone. One of his drawings was exhibited at the prestigious annual Royal Academy exhibition in a flurry of publicity when he was 17 years old and he was commissioned as a war artist in 1919. Spare was also a magician; much like Colquhoun, his art practice was also integral to his magical practice. As part of that practice, he developed a technique of drawing that might best be described as a form of spirit possession. We might usefully term his automatic practice as taking the 'left-hand path' of art (in a literal sense for those normally right-handed, as well as in a magical sense). Spare wrote a short essay outlining the technique, entitled 'Notes on Automatic Drawing', published in the British Art magazine *FORM* in 1916 and later published in *The Book of Automatic Drawing* (2005). He writes,

> An automatic scribble of twisting and interlacing lines permits the germ of an idea in the subconscious mind to express, or at least to suggest, itself to consciousness. From this mass of procreative shapes, full of fallacy, a feeble embryo of an idea may be selected and trained by the artist to full power. By these means, may the profoundest depths of memory be drawn upon and the spring of instinct tapped. (2005, n.p.)

This technique requires the artist to draw without looking, without intention; it can be done in the dark, and often with the non-dominant hand. This is about initiating a loss of control, working against its usual exercise in the drawing process. It allows rhythm and gesture to lead, and line to be made for its own sake. He tells us,

> The hand must be trained to work freely and without control, by practise in making simple forms with a continuous involved line without afterthought, i.e. its intention should just escape consciousness. Drawings should be made by allowing the hand to run freely with the least possible deliberation. [...] The mind in a state of oblivion, without desire towards reflection or pursuit of materialistic intellectual suggestions. [...] By this means sensation may be visualised. (2005: n.p.)

Spare's automatic drawings scribe into being fantastical, magical, and elemental creatures. There is an othered quality about them, seeming ecstatic in their apparently moving state, in alignment with the process which Spare evolved to produce them. Spare's magical and automatic practice was developed independently from, but alongside, the automatism advocated, and perhaps better known, within André Breton's (1896–1966) first Surrealist manifesto of 1924. It was through this call to automatic arms that Colquhoun came to develop her emergent methods, and with some select others in the movement, that became a distinctly occult art. Tapping the unconscious was for Breton a leading aim of Surrealism: his manifesto advocates 'Psychic automatism in its pure state, by which one proposes to express – verbally, by means of the written word, or in any other manner – the actual functioning of thought. Dictated by thought, in the absence of any control exercised by reason, exempt from any aesthetic or moral concern' (Danchev 2011,

247). Tessel M. Bauduin argues that 'artists were attracted to automatism because it appeared to be a means to achieve artistic freedom' (2015, 432). The search for authentic, personal creativity is the foundation of Surrealism, even though many also demonstrated hard-worn virtuosity. In his paper 'The Occult and the Visual Arts', Bauduin (2015) helpfully demonstrates that many 'Modernist' artists looked to occultism to inform their practice and working ethos, citing Kandinsky, Mondrian as well as Wagner. Such artists looked to sacred geometry, dreams, and the power of juxtaposition for their inspiration. Leonora Carrington, Max Ernst, Hilma af Klint, and Ithell Colquhoun each also added to that mix deep engagement with occult and esoteric arts to quicken their ability to invoke the Other and the unseen. In this allegiance, Gothic becomes Surrealism's fetishised bedfellow. It was only Colquhoun however that used real places, predominantly Cornwall, to cast her animistic spells of deep enchantment.

Colquhoun drew on many different automatic methods in her visual art as well as in her poetry and fiction, some of her own in invention, others devised by Max Ernst. Her early poems are collectively produced chain poems – working like an exquisite corpse with words, written down, folded over, and passed to another to include the next line (i.e. 'Question and Answer Foursome'). Her later poems are sole-authored and are 'hymns to the physical and spiritual aspects of desire, to corporeal and mystical unity' (Shillitoe 2010, 36). Colquhoun writes, 'I think a poem is floating in the ether and it is more or less by hazard that it condenses in some particular language' (cited in Shillitoe 2010 33); even while she 'translates' the poem into language for a wider audience, its prior existence she opines is autonomous to authorship. Automatism is therefore very much at the centre of her creative ethos. Her novella *The Goose of Hermogenes* (published in 1961 yet based on earlier writings (see Shillitoe, website and Hale 2012, 314)), is broadly a collage with structure-building thematic devices derived from the symbolic language of alchemy. Given that the novella has been described as 'Female Gothic' and as a *roman noir*, it is of no small interest to our study of Gothic Kernow. Arranged in short chapters with titles taken from Alchemical processes, the novel has an allegorical cast, and it invokes a magical or spiritual initiation moving towards what we might call, to appropriate a term from Deleuze and Guattari, 'becoming woman' (1980). Laced through with esoteric symbolism, it is a story of a woman coming into her sexuality and desire. Colquhoun consistently kept a dream diary and is likely to have mobilised its contents as part of her automatic methodology. As a first-person narrative, the heroine speaks intimately to the reader of her experiences while staying on an enchanted island that is the domain of her magician uncle who seeks to steal her jewels. Time and space loop and lace through the novel, mirroring the distortions of linearity that we accept as normal while experiencing a dream. The island itself is a collaged space, sometimes Mediterranean and at others seemingly referencing the Scilly Isles, a small group of islands that sit 26 miles off the far south-western tip of the Cornish coast which is marked out as 'Other' to the mainland by its semi-tropical flora, a result of a gulf-stream climate where frost is rare (vis. Summerisle of *The Wicker Man* (1973)). In this and other elements, the novella references Shakespeare's *The Tempest*. It is worth noting that the Scilly Isles are also presented as a magical 'othered' and sexualised space in du Maurier's short story 'East Wind' (2011).

The theme of transformation is core to the novel: becoming woman allied to the process of transformation inherent in alchemical practice and symbolic language. Mutability, emblemised through the conjoining of opposites is the key to unlocking creativity and transcendence. This then is a novel about creative forces and freedom, allied to gender, sexuality, and desire. Automatism is its method as a generative, pregnant, and unpredictable process. It might apply to the use of 'found materials', as in her 'throwaways' (made from food packaging and the like) as well as to her use of collage, decalcomania (pressing paper into wet paint), or stillomancy (folding paper over into ink or wet paint), drawing blind, or, Colquhoun's own invention, parsemage (pigment or dust sprinkled on water and then paper laid on it, as used in marbling). Her pluralist approach to automatism is itself a form of creative practice, as she writes, 'Does not all inspiration come from the multitudinous abyss' ('Children of the Mantic Stain' 2019, 254). Colquhoun often yokes a given method to magical invocations of the elements with techniques devised to work with the nature of different elements or producing distinctive forms; decalcomania for example producing forms relevant to landscape, foliage, or marine life (ibid., 252).

This was a topic that Colquhoun wrote about in a range of different short-form essays, including the 'Manic Stain', 'A Canvas in the Wind',' Children of the Mantic Stain' (where she lists various techniques), and 'Notes on Automatism' (collected by Shillitoe in *Medea's Charms*, 2019). One of the attractions of automatic practice implied in these essays is that what is generated is an 'open text'. This is also clear from her eponymous essay (republished in *Medea's Charms*, 2019) on the meanings of her painting 'Dance of the Nine Opals' (1942) with its 'impacted strata of meaning' layers of meanings that are open for viewers and readers to 'scry' within. The symbolic, enigmatic, and open text, derived from the hermetic nature of Alchemy, applies across Colquhoun's practice; Gothic is put into that service in her work. In her hands, with her pen, Cornwall becomes a more mystical and magical place – she brings hermetic meaning to it, she is possessed by it, and her 'psychomorphological' conjures into being a wellspring of creativity. As a magician-artist, she brings together opposites and thus works under the sign of the hermaphrodite. In this, she balances and enhances the automatic issue with a conscious shaping and intention. In this, she is both medium and magician, male and female, receptor and shaper. Importantly, automatism allows her to tap into the (imagined perhaps) energies and spirits of place in lieu of representational realism. As a form of possession, automatism becomes a Gothic mode of practice that connects very deeply to the spirits and elementals of a place, to its Genius Loci (a concept we shall return to at the very end of this book). In this, we depart from Amy Hale's lucid and informed account of Colquhoun's use of automatism, which she regards 'different from, mediumistic automatism' (2012, 310). It is in our view entirely mediumistic in nature. However, Colquhoun uses all her faculties to bring out that communion and transform a grubby mark into a rich and polyvalent text, as is evident in her account of the *Dance of the Nine Opals*. As Hale notes of her poetry, 'The idea of her automatic poetry was to bring order from the random, but order that was ultimately instructive about the nature of the universe and, in this case, alchemical duality' (2012, 312). Colour choices for example served a specific magical and optical purpose (Hale 2012, 311) making use of ritual use of colour as developed by the magical society The Golden Dawn or in Aleister Crowley's tables of correspondences (published in *Liber 777*). But also using colour optically as laid out in the colour wheel by Bauhaus artist Johannes Itten. Hale also tells us that 'Ozenfant was responsible for progressing colour theory in Britain and his influence can most likely be seen in Colquhoun's focus on scientific blending of colour and the effects of colours in proximity to one another' (2012, 316). Colour then is not simply arranged around a scheme of pleasantries – it is purposed magically and esoterically to affect transformation and transcendence. It is set to possess and enchant the viewer and artist alike and is used to show how the land is as vital and pulsing as the body. The context of automatism is therefore key to unlocking the Gothic caste of Colquhoun's Cornish-infused work and to understand her communion with her imaginary Kernow.

Legacies and Lineages: '... And the Stones Were Awake'

From the poem 'Minerals of Cornwall, Stones of Cornwall' by Peter Redgrove

It might be too over sensationalised to say that Cornwall is a land of mystics, witches, and shamen, but as we have seen in this chapter, there is a good deal of art practice that has some relationship with these various occult practices. There are many recent artists not mentioned above, notably, sculpture Tim Shaw (RA). His 15-foot bronze *Drummer* sculpture erected in 2011 has stood controversially in a square in Truro's shopping centre, the region's one (small) 'city'. A powerfully built naked man balances precariously on a sphere, energetically beating a large drum with two hands. This is an extraordinarily pagan piece of municipal sculpture; Shaw's drummer is not only an ecological call to arms but is also in the act of conducting a potent fertility rite. The generative power of sex, nature, and the Cornish landscape is also the subject of Peter Redgrove's poetry and his writings with Penelope Shuttle, the later works such as *The Black Goddess* (1987), focused on our unconscious senses and invisible forces, and *The Wise Wound* (1978), which sought to redress the pervasive idea that menstruation is a curse. Redgrove's poetry might allude to the archetypal, but it is also very localised with some poems referring to Cornish beaches, such as here 'The Moon Disposes: Perranporth Beach' and 'An Idea of Entropy on Maenporth Beach'. More recently, 'fine art' occult publishers, Scarlet Imprint have found their base in Cornwall. Established in 2007 by Alkistis Dimech and Peter Grey, they aim to publish work that 'inspires our contemporaries and supports the ongoing resurgence in magic and esotericism'. Their work connects strongly with that Colquhoun, and in Grey's article 'Rewilding Witchcraft' (2019), we hear an echo of her animist disposition. 'Witchcraft is profoundly animist and this means we have responsibilities to fulfil' (46). Grey uses animist as an ecological call to arms, reminding us that 'the fate of all things are in our hands' (39).

Artists painting Cornwall's coasts, moors, and ancient monuments can often converge with the Gothic simply because of the nature of the terrain. While artists such as Ben Nicholson and others in the Newlyn School have been compelled to engage with the bright light and geometries of St Ives, others have instead romanced more actively Kernow's dark hollows, bleak hillsides, lonely ancient chapels, stones, churchyards, and granite farmsteads, as well as its unforgiving geologies. David Bomberg (1890–1957) for example was inspired to paint the area around Zennor, an area of Cornwall where granite-studded moorland is divided erratically by ancient stone hedges and the land falls abruptly away to sheared off cliff faces that are constantly battered by raging seas. Bomberg's *Farm by the Sea* (1947) was painted with great vigour with sweeping swathes of deep red and indigo blue. This lends the painting a strong, immediate, and kinetic sense of Zennor as an othered place that lies outside of both human timescale and agencies. His gestural response to the terrain is exclamatory, a physical reaction proclaiming both awe and the impossibility of representing it. While Bomberg's work has never been regarded by art historians as Gothic, the Gothic is therefore clearly present in his Cornwall-based work not just in terms of content but also through his highly physical and soul-shaking response to the captivating and intimidating landscape. This art-making comes out of a sense of horror generated by the

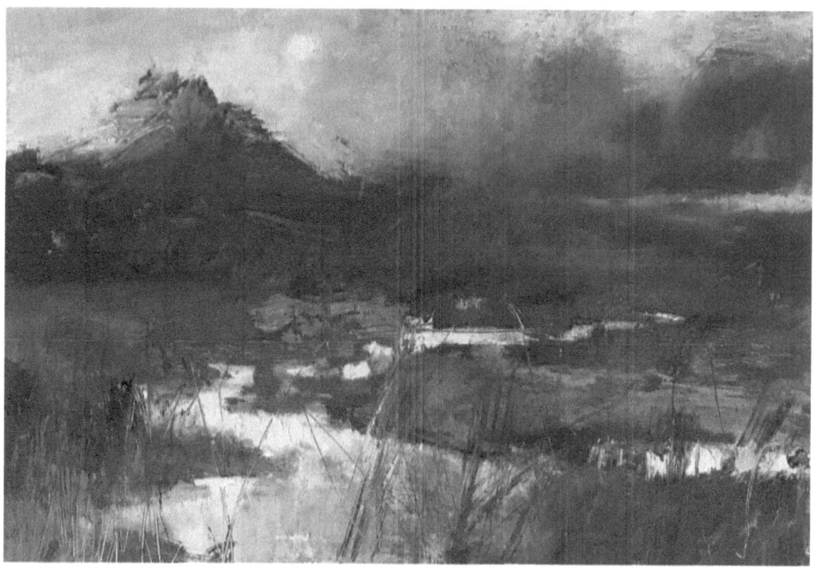

Figure 11 *Carn Galva* by Jill Eisele (2020). Oil on paper. By permission of the artist.

sheer in-human scale of Cornwall's incredible geological plenitude. The problem then is that if we see Gothic simply as a genre, we miss out on this rich Gothic strata that lurk within fine art and experimental engagement with Cornwall.

Such 'acts of making' have then a strong Gothic dimension. To use a more recent example, Cornish landscape *en pleine air* painter Jill Eisele has developed a painting process that involves swiftly laying down multiple layers of paint and pigment to generate incidents of happenstance. This enables murky darks to play against intense stabs of bright colour; thick and thin paint sit cheek-by-jowl in an intense engagement with the play of light as atmosphere and form. Eisele is thereby able to generate wild, blustery images of turbulent seas and windswept moors that run counter to the human-tamed pastoral. While her output is very different from the concerns of Colquhoun, and closer perhaps in style to Scottish painter Joan Eardley's landscapes, there is a shared lineage of creating multiple instances of incidence and happenstance through the interaction of pigments and mediums. This is in conjunction with a deep understanding of how to create form using paint and make the best use of the unintended. As seen in Figure 11, this is painting as an act of passion and perhaps can even be regarded as a form of elemental possession; Eisele becomes a witch casting her pigmented spells in full ritual connection with granite cliffs, furious seas, and horizontal weather.

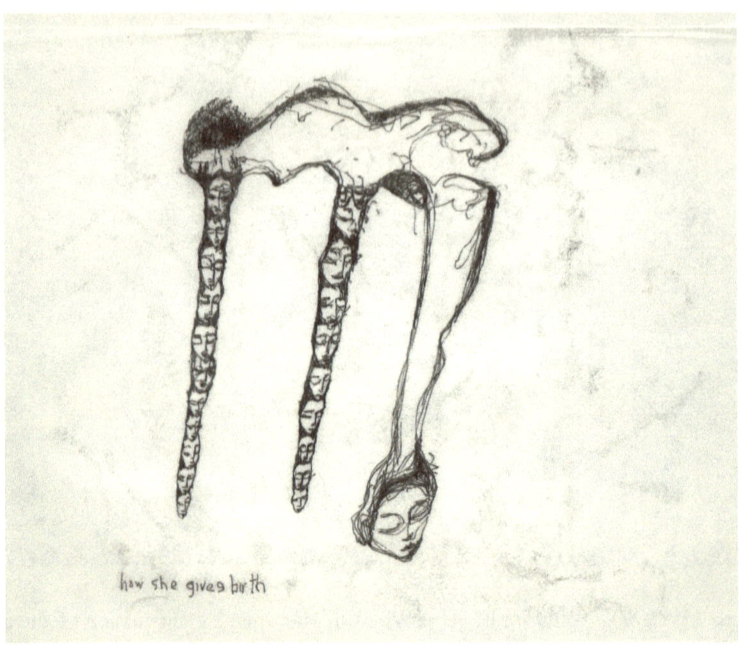

Figure 12 *How She Gives Birth with Her Blood Knowing* by Kate Walters (2016). Monotype on Sumi-e paper. By permission of the artist.

Referring to twentieth-century British landscape painters, such as John Craxton, Keith Vaughan, Robert Colquhoun, and John Minton, Christopher Neve suggests that, 'The weight of feeling placed on the landscape by so-called New Romantics makes it an unsafe place to be' (2020, 145). This also chimes with the folk and eco-horror of du Maurier, where the landscape is rendered sentient and generates vengeance, best exemplified by the short stories 'The Birds' and 'East Wind'. Eisele's darker landscapes, particularly those made around 2019 and 2020, lean towards eco-horror and reflect her ecological fears and concerns, but others lean towards the type of otherness that is found in Colquhoun landscapes. Colquhoun's approach to landscape painting drew on elements of both eco and folk horror, but their use was driven by a need to create a form of generative otherness that sought to provide spiritual and hermeneutic sustenance through a fusion of body, soul, and place. Like Bomberg's Zennor work, Eisele too seeks sustenance through a fusion with place through gestural application of paint. The body is therefore thoroughly implicated in the automatic process: emotional responses become gestural, even hieratic, in the act of laying down paint while faced with a living and moving landscape. The Neo-Romantics that Neve calls on, and particularly

Minton, were, by contrast, masters of facility and minutiae; nothing was left to chance — their magic was of a different order not suited to Kernow's mysteries.

Colquhoun's legacy in terms of generative method and earth-mysteries thematics can be seen in the work of a variety of subsequent works by artists breathing and working in Cornwall. Born in Sweden and moving to St. Ives in 1958, Monica Sjöö (1938–2005) brings Colquhoun's Earth Mysteries centre stage. Focused on Neolithic monuments, spirals, and ancient images of Goddesses, the female generative body is linked to the landscape with an explicit feminist intention. 'God Giving Birth', for example, was deemed obscene by the Mayor of St Ives when it was exhibited there in 1970, an event that prompted her into a more radical form of feminism. Like Colquhoun, Sjöö sought to represent unseen energies through linearly expressed concentric circles echoing those found in prehistoric art and evoking waveforms or ripples in a pool; Colquhoun often also used such devices to express the contours of 3-dimensional forms, for example in the rock-legs of *Scylla* (1938). Colquhoun's landscape drawings of the Nine Maidens stone circle also fuse earth energies with female bodies, a configuration found and expanded upon in many of Sjöö's drawings. A montage of her drawings formed the front cover of *Voices of the Goddess: A Chorus of Sybils* (1990) edited by Caitlin Matthews, a book focused on feminist spirituality through a celebration of the procreative female body. Sjöö's connection with Colquhoun is thematic rather than in method, however. By contrast, Kate Walters's work can be seen as a more fully rounded and individually articulated development of Colquhoun's legacy. This is apparent in Walters's themes and in the types of methods she often uses to create her work. In all these cases the resonance with Gothic is found in their subtle art magic which becomes a communion with hidden forces and energies that are channelled through the Cornish landscape.

As with many of the painters addressed in this chapter, Kate Walters (b. 1958) is an artist that came from 'up-country', as the locals call the rest of the UK, settling in Cornwall as a place to develop her practice. Much of her work is figurative and focused on the human body and its generative power. It also often depicts the body in relation to animals such as deer and horses. Connecting human ontology to the natural world is integral to the work, a thematic that integrates with Walters' training as a Shaman, evident in the composite figuration of Figure 12. Hers is an art practice that like Colquhoun has magic in its very fabric – seeking to heal our broken relationship with nature through a symbolic distillation of embodied being. As a shamanic 'hollow bone' (bird's bones are hollow to enable them to fly), she becomes a conduit for the energies of creation, connecting the material with the spirit world. This symbolic and alchemical (in magical and Jungian senses) work draws deep from Cornwall's primeval substrates as channelled through the generative body. Throughout her work, there are images of sustenance and nurture through the milk of the breast and the umbilicus, of birthing and, more recently, of acts of sexual cojoining – a response to the hiatus in touch perhaps that we have experienced through restrictions in place to contain the COVID-19 pandemic. Walters's work does not represent the landscape as an externalised other, and Cornwall is never directly represented in her work (she seems to have to go away from Cornwall to Scotland to be able to represent the landscape, as seen in her *Shetland Sketchbooks* (2019)). Instead, hers is work that sees an enraptured engagement with subtle bodies of earth, human and creature, all of which are connected and in the act of becoming. This is not about place in the way that we see in Eisele's landscapes; Walters's is not focused on such a localised and immediate approach but instead, her process is more archetypally interiorised in nature. Because of this, she is able to explore the generative in a more nuanced and receptive way; rather than working through gesture, she works automatically using rhythm and channelling drawing through the generative organs of her body. Her use of shamanic drumming and trance as a means of altering consciousness becomes her generative method for tuning into the subtle spirit world of archetypal forces. Like Colquhoun, she works with subtle bodies of her materials to open up their sensitivity as literally mediums to a spirit world. In many ways, her work can be described as an aesthetic of both becoming and otherness. The work published in *Mysterious Tissue: Of Flesh and Stars* (2011) for example made use of the fluid dynamics of watercolour to birth images of female forms that are often sinuously connected to animals or trees. Colquhoun and Walters share therefore an animistic and generative worldview that informs their writing, poetry, and image-making, as well as sharing ontological, magical, and spiritual concerns. Theirs is certainly a brand of Cornish Gothic strange-making, not so much fiction perhaps, but more than that as it is where the imaginary is purposed as magic to manifest real and tangible effects.

CHAPTER 3

STRANGE FOLK: *FOLK HORROR CULTURES, RITUAL,* AND *WITCHING WOMEN*

Chapter 2 examined engagement with the occult and the sublime Cornish landscape in the context of visual culture and fine art practice. In this chapter, we focus on a unique blend of folk culture and Gothic evidenced in fiction-based representations of the region. In addition to an examination of the structural, semantic, and thematic uses of ritual and sacrifice, we will turn our investigation to the roles that women often play in these fictions, in particular in relation to the performance of magic and rituals connected with fertility and the sea, and thus to power. The libidinal and embodied connections that we have discussed in the previous chapters are therefore extended here into the domain of Folk Horror.

The chapter addresses the thematic and generative aspects of Folk Horror in relation to Cornwall both real and imaginary. The first main section, 'Rites and Rituals of the Strange Folk', evaluates the role that the festival, ritual, and sacrifice play in the iconography and structure of Cornish Folk Horror. Using David Pinner's novel *Ritual* (2011), written in 1967, as a hub text, we compare it with Susan Cooper's children's novel *Greenwitch* (1973), and the film, *The Wicker Man* (1973). Demonstrating that 'wrongness' has been present in Cornish based folk horrors, such as in *Ritual* and *Straw Dogs* (1971), long before the TV series *True Detective* (Packer and Stoneman, 2018), we will reveal how Cornwall's folk culture often plays to incipient fears of otherness and the Other. We will evaluate the value of ritual sacrifice for Gothic fiction in terms of narrative structure, spectacle, empowerment, and sensationalism. As we will see, ritual and sacrifice are integral to the fictions that we address, raising interesting questions about the ontology not only of Gothic as a framing device but also around the fraught relationship between natural forces and human agency. Cornwall plays a role in this as both mise en scène and animistic agent. Rituals and sacrifice are used to stage the other and the unconscionable, yet they also function thematically, psychologically, and magically as (rational and irrational) techniques for controlling the other. We then turn to examine the perennial use and constitutional presence of 'Sea Rites and Witching Women' in Cornish folk horror. We will see that in imaginings of Cornwall, the Gothic and Folk Horror become intertwined with the landscape as well as with various forms of paganism, localized myths, and legends. This potent mixture is what makes Cornish Gothic unique.

As might be expected, all the texts that we address here are set fully or partially in Cornwall or which have a strong connection to it. The films and novels we go on to discuss each have a strong claim on 'Folk Horror'; some sit plumb in the centre of the category, with *The Wicker Man* and *Ritual* as definitional of the genre, while others have a more indirect lineage, as with *Greenwitch.* One of our core arguments here is to demonstrate that 'Folk Horror' is in common usage in fiction set in Cornwall and is operative in texts of a far broader nature than those that are usually cited. In terms of our methodological approach, it is worth noting that we do not regard texts generally as discrete or hermetically sealed. As is implicit in the analysis conducted throughout this book, we argue that they are part of a wider socio-cultural 'ecology' that is integral to the ontology of Gothic Kernow. Our comparative, cross-medial approach emerges directly from a conception that sees the meaning of texts as emergent through their actuation in culture. As Mikko Lehtonen puts it in his book *The Cultural Analysis of Texts,* 'meanings and social relationships are [...] tightly entwined with each other' (2000, 14). This approach, therefore, allows our chapter to address 'strange folk' in broader terms, looking beyond the texts to, for example, rhetoric and practices of folk ritual, tourism, language, agency and determinism, and gender. In addition, we will conduct ourselves in this approach through conceptual frames and schema provided by both Gothic and contemporary concerns; namely, figurations of otherness (nature, women, monstrosity, the prehistorical past), economies of transgression, dichotomies, and anxieties around agency and determinism, as well as the conflicted nature of our relationship with the environment.

Rites and Rituals of the Strange Folk

While there is a large body of academic work on the film *The Wicker Man* that is focused on its role in cinematic history and around Folk Horror, its cross-over with the Gothic is rather thinly explored and few have addressed the film's 'parent' text, David Pinner's novel *Ritual.* This novel is set entirely in Cornwall, and it provided the inspiration for the script of *The Wicker Man.* In the introduction to *Ritual,* Bob Stanley notes that after buying the film rights to the novel, Anthony Schaffer spent a weekend with Robert Hardy 'brainstorming until the skelton

[sic] of a storyline was ready' (2011, n.p.). The story that emerged had tangible cross-overs with *Ritual*, from the Puritan policeman investigating the death of a young girl in a remote location among 'strange folk' to 'clear parallels between other characters' (ibid). And Stanley contends that 'Although Schaffer said he wasn't adapting *Ritual* this is something of a trick' (ibid). In addition to a close and comparative analysis of these two texts and the role of 'folk' ritual and sacrifice played within them, we demonstrate that the folk horror texts set in Cornwall are, in fact, a perfect place from which to delve deeper into the scope of what has been called 'Folk Horror'. A core argument then of this chapter is that Cornwall, as a fictional device, has played a constitutional role in the development of a generic folk horror grammar that Adam Scovell (2017) and others formulate. Bringing a Gothic lens on such texts has the advantage of developing and fuelling the Folk Horror concept to include a wider, more generalist, and permeable cultural remit.

Archaeology

Typified elements of Folk Horror are widely deployed in representations of Cornwall (and not only in those that are fiction-based). An examination of Folk Horror elements reveals that they have their roots in historical and archaeological sources, providing productive ground for fictional depictions of a region, its people, and landscape. We are therefore looking at a far more pervasive formation of Folk Horror than a cluster of films made in the United Kingdom in the 1970s, generally as well as in relation to Gothic Cornwall. As a staple of Folk Horror, ancient sources are widely referenced, explicitly so in *The Wicker Man* of 1973 and then, in turn, inherited in *The Third Day* (2020), as well as in the depiction of Uppsala sacrificial rites in the TV series *Vikings* (series 1, Ep. 8, 2013) or in the film *Midsommar* (2019). In historical terms, Roman writers such as Julius Caesar (BC 100–44), writing on the religion of the Gauls, and Tacitus's (AD 56–c. 120) biography of his father-in-law Gnaeus Julius Agricola, who was Roman Governor of Britain, are responsible for creating some of the key tropes of Folk Horror, its memetic qualities fuelled by lurid descriptions of the barbarity of northern pagan sacrificial rites and ritual. Christian writers such as German Chronicler Adam of Bremen, writing in the eleventh century, and Snorri Sturluson, Icelandic historian-poet writing in the twelfth century, refer to extensive human sacrifice at a temple in Uppsala, including that of nine men (nine is a number sacred to Odin), recalled in the film *Midsommar*. Subsequent engravings based on these writings and made in the seventeenth century presented elements of these writings as arresting visual images, designed for popular consumption, notably referencing various and strange means of human sacrifice, as for example 'The Wicker Colossus of the Druids' published in 1771 (similarly images of witches and witch cults).

All these early examples of Folk Horror were designed to heat the blood and serve, alongside myth and folk tales, as an impetus for more recent examples of Folk Horror fiction based in Northern Europe. In all cases, those of whom they wrote were positioned as occupying the margins, as an uncivilised or heathen other, even if, as Walter Burkert writes, 'animal-sacrifice was an all-pervasive reality in the ancient world' (1983, 9). Add to this heady, gory mix, James Frazer's accounts of sacrifice, ritual, and magic (which he describes as erroneously functional in purpose as tools in the practice of farming and husbandry) were published as *The Golden Bough* in 1890. This and the following threads to the tale, all work their magic on the construction and credibility of Folk Horror. Ploughing in the same field as Frazer, there was renewed interest in 'ceremonial' magic, typified by Victorian magical order, The Golden Dawn (1887–1903), and an enthusiasm for the idea that pre-Christian pagan witch cults have been kept alive secretly as set out by Margaret Alice Murray's *The Witch-Cult in Western Europe* published in 1921 and Gerald Gardner's *The Meaning of Witchcraft* in 1959. With the formation of the Folklore Society in 1878, the stage is set for rite-based Folk Horror to become an integral part of Gothic fiction, from Arthur Machen's short story *The Great God Pan* (1890), E. F. Benson's *The Temple* (1924), through to Sylvia Townshend Warner's *Lolly Willowes* (1926) and Ari Aster's *Midsommar*. In this context, remote, rural places like Cornwall were no longer just visually 'picturesque' or romantically sublime but places where the old ways persisted. Such locations of remaindered primitivist pagan practices were ripe for reanimation by folklore hobbyists, of which Cornwall has had many, including, Rev. RS Hawker (1803–1975), novelist Anna Elizabeth Bray (1790–1883), William Bottrell (1816–1881), Nellie Slogett (1850–1923), and Cecil Williamson (1909–1999). All this creative and often appropriative excitement provided the necessary kindling for stoking the fires of Folk Horror and Cornwall's substantial stake within it.

Cornwall certainly has a good share of ritual-based festivals to keep the pagan fires burning. To name a few: Padstow's Mayday (Beltane) 'Obby 'Oss'; The Furry Dance festival ('fer' feast or fair in Cornish) in Helston on Flora Day; the 8th May (unless that falls on a Sunday), Golowan fires on hilltops across the region (Cornish for Midsummer); Padstow's Mummer's Day (known controversially as Darkie's Day) on Boxing Day or New Year's Day. More recent contemporary pagan inventions include the torchlit procession named Montol, held in Penzance on the night of winter solstice since 2007. Some antique perhaps, but there is certainly a sense of the antique in both

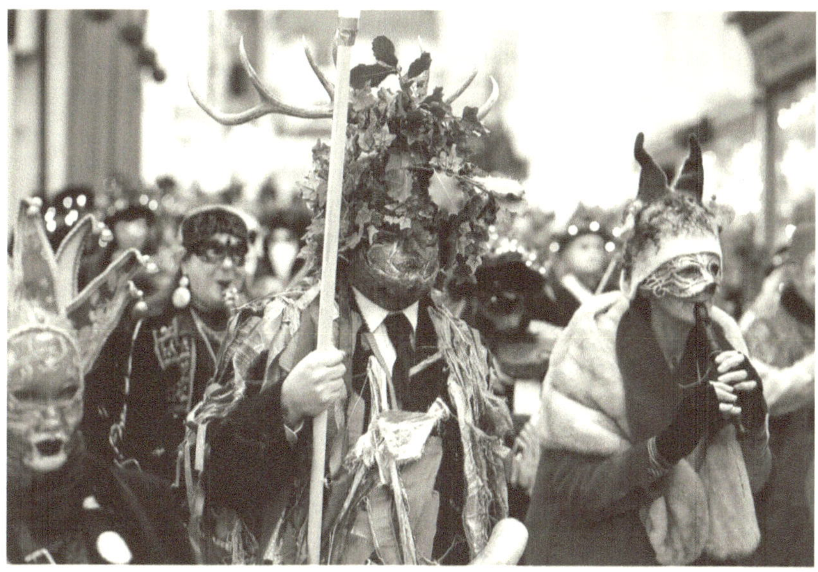

Figure 13 'Montol Festival. Penzance. Midwinter Festival 21 December'. Creative Commons.

revivalist and neo-pagan interest in keeping up these 'traditions'; part-fuelled by a need to play to the tourist gaze and of course to support a shared imaginary rendering of Cornwall as a place still connected to the deep pre-Christian past.

Some of these festivals (see Figure 13 for a Cornish example) play a role in the imagined folk horror rituals of the sort that appear in David Pinner's *Ritual.* This is also the case with Pinner's more recent e-book, *The Wicca Woman* (2014), a novel that is embedded in an imagined pre-Christian pagan culture and, in an echo-chamber of mutual intertextuality, which makes clear reference to *The Wicker Man.* Very little has been written about Pinner's seminal novel (nor its sequel), bar the odd footnote in the many critical engagements with the original and reworkings of *The Wicker Man* (i.e. Franks et al., 2006; Hardy and Shaffer, 2000; Brown, 2000; Aloi, 2016). Pinner has had a strong engagement with Gothic in his plays and novels, and along with his focus on Cornwall, his work is therefore a fitting addition to this book, and to Gothic and Folk Horror criticism generally; his approach is more grotesque, expressionist, and satirical than in the 'Wicker' reworkings which are more widely known. Given the centrality of rites and rituals within both of his novels addressed here, alongside Cornwall's culture and in its fictional representation, these texts provide the chapter's nodes. We will start with the ways in which rites and rituals are defined and deployed. In so doing, we have recourse to a concept that we discussed in some detail in Chapter 2: animism.

Ritual in Theory and Practice

In *Totem and Taboo*, Freud writes, 'Animism is a system of thought. It does not merely explain a particular phenomenon but allows us to grasp the whole universe as a single entity' (1990, 134), and in the development of an animistic point of view,

> the practical need for controlling the world around them must have played its part. So, we are not surprised to learn that, hand-in-hand with an animistic system, there went a body of instructions upon how to obtain mastery of men, beasts and things, or rather over their spirits. These instructions go by the name of 'sorcery' or 'magic'. (1990, 135)

In this schema, magic becomes the technique of animism and is therefore intimately connected to ritual. This formulation was also in play in Colquhoun's approach to art as a form of magical ritual, as set out in the previous chapter. In a generalist sense, ritual is a term, however, in which very many things have been and are invested, framed as it is by different disciplines and interests. While this chapter is not the place to examine different rhetorical and disciplinary uses of the term ritual in any depth, it is important to provide a brief overview of divergent meanings as a means of providing a grounding for our discussion of rites and rituals in the context of Folk Horror generally and more specifically within *Ritual*, *The Wicker Man*, and *Greenwitch*. For a good overview of ritual across disciplines, see Stephenson (2011).

Broadly regarded as both sociological and psychological in nature, ritual is often seen as a pivot around which human beings interact with their world and each other. Following Émile Durkheim (1912/1995), anthropologists and sociologists tend to focus on the role ritual plays as a means of unifying society, through shared practices and meanings. As Stephenson puts it, for Durkheim, it is a case of 'no ritual; no society'; ritual produces social unity and 'effervescence' (2011, 40). We should note from this that rites and rituals are part of all societies and are not confined to Dennis Wheatley-esque black magic rituals or rural micro-cultures, wherein they othered. Within psychology, and particularly psychoanalysis, interest in rites and rituals is focused instead on repeated behaviours and compulsions as enacted by individuals. Rituals in the form of public ceremonies and festivals (rites) have been regarded as both rebellious, as with Bakhtin's Carnivalesque, and as a means of naturalising and mystifying authority (Gluckman, 1965). Victor Turner (1982) argues that ritual is culturally performative and his work has often been explored in the context of drama; by contrast, in 'Ritual Theory, Ritual Practice' (1992), Catherine Bell argues that ritual is a tool used by those in power and with authority to dominate and coerce. Ritual then has been sited theoretically in the sacred and every day, the ancient and modern, the political and religious, the personal and collective. With such proliferation of functions, contexts, and meanings, the concept starts to sound rather nebulous and confusing. Most theorists from whatever disciplinary background do, however, think of it as an 'action' and many as an act of communication. The festive rituals active in Cornwall today hover between tradition and fiction, yet as they are actualised through performance, they demonstrate how the enactment of rites bridge a gap between the real and the fantastic. This sounds all quite civilised, but at what point do repeated behaviours and folk customs become allied to blood sacrifice? Is it simply a titillating and sensational fictional device that is convenient for Gothic monetisation? In conjunction with ritual, sacrifice too has been identified as another 'node' that is integral to human development. Walter Burkert, for example, argues that for all classical civilizations, ritual and blood sacrifice are inseparable, 'animal-sacrifice was an all-pervasive reality in the ancient world' (1983, 9), and he places sacrifice at the heart of all religion, 'sacrificial killing is the basic experience of the sacred. Homo Religiosis acts and attains self-awareness as Homo Necans [killing]' (1983, 3). This is important to note if we are to understand where Folk Horror originates and why it has such imaginative potency and fictional pull. Sacrifice starts to look like civilisation's shadow, an estranged source of the vitality inherent in the Other.

While ritual has been identified within everyday behaviour, it is also often described spatially as apart from the everyday (Turner's liminal space). In *Homo Ludens* (1955), Johan Huizinga writes,

> Just as there is no formal difference between play and ritual, so the 'consecrated spot' cannot be formally distinguished from the play-ground. The arena, the card-table, the magic circle, the temple, the stage, the screen, the tennis court, the court of justice, etc, are all in form and function play-grounds, i.e. forbidden spots, isolated, hedged round, hallowed, within which special rules obtain. All are temporary worlds within the ordinary world, dedicated to the performance of an act apart. (10)

This 'apartness' provides an integral element of Folk Horror, structurally and thematically, and makes Cornwall a resonant setting by virtue of its geographical distance. David Hanlan, the Cromwellian copper of Pinner's *Ritual*, comes to

Cornwall to investigate his intuition that a ritual murder has taken place; told in the third person, the reader follows him for most of the novel, making of us with him an outsider. This is also the case with *The Wicker Man.* Sergeant Howie, the Christian copper, flies to the island of Summerisle (an imaginary place but located in the real world off the western coast of Scotland), and as with *Ritual*, the reader is aligned with his journey. In keeping with this, Dani and Christian travel from the United States to rural Sweden in *Midsommar*, as do Sam and Jess in *The Third Day*. In each of these examples, in tandem with the main character, we are positioned as the interloper. We may not wish to be and might instead be drawn to identify with the pagans, but that would be to go counter to the intended interpolative schema of all these fictions, where point of view and identification are meant to intersect – even if this is overturned later. The otherness and transgressive value of these imagined pagan cultures are dependent on our taking up this position of the outsider.

A key element of Folk Horror is the use of real-world geographical locations that each come conveniently pre-loaded with well-known strange significations. This realist manoeuvre helps to shore up the conditions of suspension of disbelief and further encourages the breakdown of the safety net provided by the frame of representation/fiction that is integral to horror's project and potency. The real world rural 'midsummer' ritual traditions are therefore invoked to lend greater credibility, richness, and resonance to these strange fictions. In so doing they overdetermine the sense that 'special rules obtain' where real space and the psychological space we carve out to engage with such fictions enable the performance of an act apart. In this, horror and tragedy share common ground; we become witnesses to horrific events that we can do nothing to change; mediation in effect becomes more transparent through the ritualised emotional economy of Folk Horror. In *Poetics*, Aristotle notes the cathartic effects of tragedy, 'an imitation of an action that is serious, complete and of a certain magnitude [...] through pity and fear effecting the proper purgation of these emotions.' To which we might add, sacrificial death acting as an encouragement towards a deeper examination of life.

It is here that we broach the psychological construction of a space where special rules obtain. This applies to the 'act' of fiction-making both for the authors of these fictions and for the central characters in these folk horror texts. It is also in this psychological dimension that Folk Horror can be seen as familial to 'weird fiction' with roots in H. P. Lovecraft's mythos (and not just in terms of strange sea-focused rituals, of which more later). In the case of each of these fictions, the sacrificial scenarios can be regarded as the central character's own overblown, hysterical (here we nod back to Phillip and Ambrose those male hysterics of Chapter 1). Hanlan, the Cromwellian Puritan, is revealed to be psychotic schizophrenic with a penchant for florid murder under the guise of hunting down ritual murderers; Howie has constructed his own martyrdom in the manner of an early Christian saint; Dani Ardor in *Midsommar* seems to have dreamed up the ritual sacrifice of her (rubbish) boyfriend, Christian Hughes; in *The Third Day*, main character Sam and academic Jess each have cause for such invention. In all this mise en abyme of hallucinations, projections and intertextual borrowings, disavowal, pretence, and dissembling, the use of game-like rites forges a deadly alliance between playfulness and ritual. In *Ritual*, *The Wicker Man*, and (at the time of writing) the most recent foray into Folk Horror, *The Third Day*, children play key roles not only in the rites themselves but also in baiting their victims. Huizinga's magic circle of games (1949) takes on a more literal meaning; far from innocent these children help to reel in their game and make of sacrifice 'child's play', helping to up the horror and transgressive ante, deliberately othering themselves, and placing the adults that encourage their lord-of-the-flies' behaviours as outside the sanctity of civilisation. Cornwall becomes Caesar's land of barbarians.

The Cornwall of *Ritual* is, therefore, presented through multiple channels as othered terrain. Only in part through the conduit of the rugged landscape, as in the romantic sensibility. Following Tacitus, it is through the isolation of its people and their continued practice of ritual sacrifice the otherness garners its full effect (even if these Cornish turn out to be far less barbarous than psychotic, perverse, puritan Hanlan). As we can see, real-world referents combine with imaginary ones, and, in the context of Folk Horror, it is ritual that most expresses the strangeness of folk.

To summarise: Folk Horror uses rites and ritual as (a) a means of stitching a text into preceding sources and practices, as demonstrated above, (b) an opportunity to thematise death as a form of dramatic spectacle, as discussed above, (c) a technique for performing magic, (d) a means of exploiting the fear and frisson of the other, and (e) as a means of connecting with an animistic landscape. Before we move on to look more specifically at the use of sea ritual and its connection with Cornish Gothic, we will linger yet a while on ritual as a means for performing magic, and the exploitation of the fear of the other. Consideration of these two areas helps us to understand not only Folk Horror as a modality but also the types of dichotomies that our key texts engage with and the ways in which they have been (diversely) interpreted. It will also provide a framework that we will use when looking more closely at the use of sea rituals later in the chapter.

Transgression and Sensationalism

Various branches of Gothic literature have used ritual and human sacrifice as a means of creating theatrical set pieces in their fictions exploiting what philosopher Roger Caillois called in 1958 'the interregnum of vertigo, effervescence, and fluidity in which all that symbolises order in the universe is temporarily abolished' (2001, 87). In terms of narratology, occult or folk culture rituals, some involving sacrifice, others simply orgies, function often as a denouement or as a staged battle between conflicting forces, as in Dennis Wheatley's novel *The Devil Rides Out* (1948). While in an anthropological sense, ritual is a bounded space where different rules apply, in the context of narrative function, they operate as dramatic motivation and pivot, as well as concluding spectacle. Ceremonial clothing, nakedness, wild cliff tops, woodland or sea-side locations, set dramatic speeches, and coordinated ritualised movements all play well to the camera in the context of visual fiction, while the structured nature and pace of ritual, along with archaic and or poetic use of magical language, play to written or spoken forms. As in anthropological usage, and in the need to garner the attention of negligent deities, fictional ritual needs to arrest the gaze. Ritual can also function narratologically as a means of establishing a hierarchy of dramatis personae, as in *The Wicker Man*, where the role of 'King' is inhabited by Lord Summerisle (Christopher Lee). This role is in keeping with its allegiance to Frazer's notion of the Dying King, as poignantly noted by Howie before his fiery demise, and incidentally, the same notion is deployed in John Boorman's film *Excalibur* (1981) where King Arthur's well-being is linked to the prosperity of the land – we should note that Arthur is conceived by magical deception in the Cornish castle, Tintagel. In its satirical modality, Pinner's *Ritual* is far less cut and dry in terms of any 'magical' hierarchy and as such departs from the Frazerian sacrificial structure. In tandem with this, there is little sense of a sanctioned social order and all roles play against themselves: Hanlan represents chaos rather than the law, the priest is sexually incontinent, and the squire dabbles in black magic. As such, in this topsy-turvydom, we can see echoes of Caillios's 'interregnum of vertigo', and it is also evident in the deliberately transgressive fluidity of sexual identity played out by various incumbents of the village.

Excluding *Midsommar*, our small group of roughly similarly dated texts, all of which have a connection to Cornwall and its apparent intrinsic paganism, are in close dialogue with an increasingly sexually 'permissive' culture, alongside an increasingly outmoded Christianity, and the collapse of the hippie ideal, often located in 1968. Cornwall seems to represent for many – artists, bohemians, and hippies in particular – a place of light and nature from which to escape received norms and expectations. However, for the sexual and sacrificial elements of the rites and rituals in Folk Horror texts to have a 'tragic' and vertiginous impact, they do also have to be presented in a transgressive light. *The Wicker Man's* Howie, and *Ritual's* Hanlan both function in their melodramatic outrage to sensationalise even the most 'natural' sexual aspects of the rituals and pagan lifestyle on display to them. Sensationalism through the frame of transgression has of course been a key weapon in the armoury of the Gothic since *The Castle of Otranto*. However, both *The Wicker Man* and *Ritual* go beyond the device by using their key characters' puritanical outrage to ask questions of whether a pagan ritualistic way of life and sexual freedom is in fact transgressive at all. Howie and Hanlan are so overblown in their disgust and outrage, as well as their sexual stoicism, that it is very hard to identify with their positions. Oddly perhaps, this offers the key to unlocking why it is that *The Wicker Man* offers itself not simply as a Folk Horror film, but also – and perhaps the greatest horror of all – as a folk horror musical.

Why so much singing? Youth interest in folk music during the late 1960s might certainly have been a tactic to pull in the typical youth crowd for horror cinema, but there is more to this than market. First, as Richard Dyer notes in *Entertainment and Utopia* (2002), the musical has a very ritualised structure and often it foregrounds a sense of community through shared songs. This echoes the use of song in *The Wicker Man*, singing collectively about sex in the inn and the whole community singing and swaying together hand-linked-to-hand while Howie burns. Throughout the film, there is a strong sense that paganised folk songs about sex, fertility, and agriculture are derived from an ancient tradition outside the pious hymns sung in church or chapel. At several points during the film, we also see Howie singing hymns in church, significantly the walls are bare, and he sings with great confident gusto. His Calvinist, puritan position references the Cromwellian legislation of the British interregnum that banned images in churches, along with dancing, maypole, or otherwise, folk festivals including Christmas, most of which were accompanied by non-religious, indigenous folk songs. As Chris Partridge writes, 'Throughout the film, the folk music is explicitly identified with the survival of a pre-Christian indigenous religion […] the use of music and dance evokes the vibrancy of nature religion and the occult over the dry formalism of mainland Calvinist theology' (2015, 513). Cornish folk song continues to have a purchase in this light, connecting back to the Cornish language and identity that was suppressed in the aftermath of the 1549 'Prayer Book' Rebellion, protesting the King's protestant edict that the nation must use an English language book of prayer and destroy religious shrines. As well as carried in folk songs, the memory of protestant puritanism is found in stories that suggest standing stones were dancers punished by God for their dancing, as with the Nine Maidens stone circle discussed in Chapter 2. *Ritual*'s Hanlan names himself Cromwellian, a puritan protestant, often seemingly in jest; however, he also bears more than a passing resemblance to Matthew Hopkins of *The Witch Finder General* (1968), a film that is set in the run up to the interregnum and based on a historical, if delusional, persona (1620–1647). In the context of the protestant reformation and the interregnum, transgression has a heightened meaning – ostracisation, torture, and martyrdom were common currency; it may explain why such histories resurface in Folk Horror and connects back to enmity between Cornwall and England.

As we have noted throughout this book, Cornwall has an outsider status. Du Maurier is often on to this in her novels and short stories, in *The Birds* for example, but in *The King's General*, it is Cornwall of the interregnum that draws her imagination, providing a space for its heroine, Honor Harris to act as such. Cornwall was split in the English Civil war (1642–1651), yet most of its powerful families sided with King and Catholicism and were presumably set against puritan rule and its abnegation of social and spiritual hierarchy. This allegiance differs from the Parliamentarian support of most of the south-west of England. Cornwall put up fierce resistance and Royalists won ground in Cornwall with the Battles of Braddock Down (1643) and Lostwithiel (1644), as well as The Gear Rout rebellion of 1648, resulting in a failed Royalist Cornish rebellion and isolated resistance persisted in West Cornwall and the Isles of Scilly. Rebellion seems entrenched in Cornish history, precipitated by its location: surrounded by sea and cut off by the Tamar Valley. The Civil War was, of course, an 'interregnum of vertigo', where the rule of God was challenged on both sides, god-sanctioned Kingship set against god-fearing puritanism; each of which had a very different notion of ritual. No wonder then the Civil war has so many links with Folk Horror (*A Field in England*, *Blood on Satan's Claw*, *Witchfinder General*, and evoked in *Ritual's* self-named Cromwellian Hanlan and the out of place out of time, Puritan Sergeant Howie).

Very little of Cornwall's history of rebellion finds its way directly into Folk Horror set in the region, bar in du Maurier. Instead, it is indirectly but powerfully present in the uses of the strangeness of Cornwall's folk where they become allied to an animistic form of paganism, that is leveraged by 'dark tourism'. This is best emblemised by Cecil Williamson's Witchcraft Museum that he brought to Boscastle in 1960, after problems with the locals at various previous locations. Williamson's museum displays folk magic, ritual, and ceremonial items that he concocted, snaffled, or had donated. With an eye to sensation and transgressive rhetoric, he labelled and displayed folk magic artefacts, placed alongside lurid dioramas of sexual sacrifice to stimulate passing tourists; the dioramas are now gone, the museum now has something of a museum-of-a-museum about it, includes far more women-centred exhibits, and is run by the Folklore Society.

To some extent the source of a view of ritual magic as transgressive practice has its roots in a protestant suspicion of ritual and festivals, associating them with Catholicism. This seems to be the basis for many fictional representations of black magic and often Folk Horror calls on black magic in representing pagan ritual – this is then a protestant conflation that in turn works for transgressive spectacle. We should more properly divide hermetic magical practice from that of folk magic. In so doing, we can see why a film like *A Dark Song* (2016), which is focused on a magical ritual, can be regarded as an occult film rather than folk horror. Much is also the case with the more satanic and conspiratorial *The Ninth Gate* (1999) and Dennis Wheatley's black magic novels, which Phil Baker posits 'did a great deal to share the popular image of occultism and satanism in twentieth century Britain [...] and reduced hermetic science to rogering virgins on altar tops' (2015, 465). *Bait* (2019) or *The Lighthouse* (2019) each draw on Folk Horror and tacitly human sacrifice. In many ways, while there is a legacy in these films left by Tacitus and Fraser, they are also much indebted to the weird fiction of H. P. Lovecraft, with all its strange rituals, dark gods, and fears of the other. Perhaps, it is worth remembering that both Maine and Cornwall are of course coastal, and it is now to the sea and the rites it demands that we turn.

Sea Rites and Witching Women

It seems, then as if the folklore and the modes of the Gothic associated with Cornwall as well as its landscape are uniquely crafted to the relatively newly identified concept of Folk Horror. Dawn Keetley argues that 'folk horror embodies an explicitly ecological world-view in which human and nature, human and nonhuman, are thoroughly imbricated. [...] Folk horror demands a critical methodology that pays attention to its actual locations – to the ways particular stone structures, rivers, valley, mountains, and border regions have dictated their own stories' (Keetley, 2020, 9–10). The rituals, real and imagined, of Cornwall all imbricate the human with the non-human, largely through the thresholds between land and sea, the supernatural and the natural. And often a productive linkage is provided by powerful women – witching women.

Isabella van Elferen states that 'Ritual is the creation of a performative twilight zone in which the sacred and secular spill over into each other; as this type of expenditure is at the heart of Gothic, rituals and rituality are frequent themes in the genre' (2013, 437). In *My Cousin Rachel*, we saw Philip semi-ritualistically burying the terrible letter from Ambrose which accused Rachel (naively assuming that what is buried will not eventually come to light), while Colquhoun ritualistically squeezed herself widdershins through the Mên-an-Tol stone.

These rituals involve the granite stone of Cornwall, part of the 'Gothic strata' we wrote about in previous chapters. However, in many of the unique modes of Cornish Gothic, the sea is at the centre of its rituals that breach the boundaries between land and ocean. In 1907, Sir Arthur Conan Doyle presents a picture of Cornwall in *Through the Magic Door* that precedes Lovecraft's more well-known geographical estrangements,

> There is something wonderful, I think, about the land of Cornwall. That long peninsula extending out into the ocean has caught all sorts of strange floating things, and has held them there in isolation until they have woven themselves into the texture of the Cornish race. [...] Yes, there is something strange, and weird, and great, lurking down yonder in the great peninsula which juts into the western sea. (22)

The entire peninsula of Cornwall is, of course, a border region, bounded as it is by the sea. In his article 'The Gothic Coast', Jimmy Packham says he 'makes the claim that the coast has long stood as a key locale in gothic writing and, by so doing, recovers a neglected feature of the gothic tradition: to the labyrinthine castle, ruined abbey, and inhospitable mountain ranges of Europe, we might add the coast as a site of gothic experience *par excellence*' (2018, 206). Packham looks at the coast as an uncanny, shifting, uncertain space where each tide threatens to uncover that which should perhaps remain beneath the waves. His focus is on the coast as an 'ecotone' – a space where two ecological zones meet and mingle – and he relates this to shifting and contested national boundaries. He states,

> The coast in gothic fiction tests the limits of the self, exposing it to the hostile, and potentially fatal, forces of a volatile environment and foreign or alien beings: monstrous creatures populate a shoreline that is symbolically and culturally the intersection of two worlds, on known and familiar, the other unknown and uninhabitable. (208)

Folk horror is always a particular kind of what might be described as 'rural Gothic' where, as Bernice Murphy argues, there is 'a symbolic reservoir of tradition and belief [...]. There must be at least some [...] kind of "mythic framework"' (2022). There is not just the irrational, or perhaps even non-sensical, violence, terror, and horror associated with examples of rural Gothic from *An American Werewolf in London* to Robert Eggers's *The Lighthouse.* Folk Horror needs its folk (i.e. Cornish villagers) to have some kind of the 'skewed belief systems and morality' identified by Adam Scovell (18). Scovell discusses the only two Hammer horror films to be set in Cornwall: *The Reptile* and *The Plague of the Zombies* (1966). Although both were filmed in Surrey, Scovell says, 'Their (admittedly visually flimsy) setting on the Cornish coast sets their tone apart from other Hammer films of the era' (84). And it is this coastal locating that forms part of Cornwall's folk horror and Gothic texts. Cornwall's landscape and identity are defined by the sea often more than the granite rocks which underlie it but which cannot provide fertile ground for farming. The sea itself is the most productive and generative part of the coastal landscape but it can also be the most destructive. And, in the Folk Horror texts set in Cornwall, the rituals performed by Cornish folk involve sacrifices made to the sea to ensure a good harvest both from the ocean and the land.

David Pinner's *Ritual* and its sequel *The Wicca Woman*, and *Greenwitch* by Susan Cooper, each place a ritual sacrifice to the sea as a core dramatic event. These rituals, performed by local Cornish folk, are older than anyone can remember, lending a strong sense of both otherness and belonging; they work with the borders of the ecotone (the sea and the land), the human and the non-human, and create spaces where the real and the fantastic commingle. Rituals to propitiate the sea, led by women, have provided fertile ground for many imaginings of Cornwall and its inhabitants. In this way, the identified eroticised relationship between creatives (du Maurier and Colquhoun, for example) and the land and sea are extended to look at the ritualisation of this libidinal and embodied connection and alchemical bond. The sea as a location for Folk Horror has most recently been exploited in Robert Eggers's *The Lighthouse* which documents the complete mental and physical undoing of two men marooned on a rock, surrounded by a raging sea. Real or not real, imagined or not, the film focuses on the disintegration of masculine identity. And as Eggers said in an interview with Katie Rife for the A. V. Club, 'nothing good happens when two men are trapped in a giant phallus'. In the novels examined here, the emphasis is different. And while masculinity is still deconstructed to the point of disintegration (especially in Pinner's work), it is the women who are able to identify with, and to some extent to placate, the sea. In all the novels, the rituals associated with the sea and fertility are communal, village affairs. Each ritual is annual, performed by all the villagers, although in each one the women take the leading roles. In Chapter 2, in relation to Colquhoun's work, we explored her work as coinciding with an 'Eco-feminist informed Gothic'. In her artwork as well as in du Maurier's *My Cousin Rachel*, the female is associated (for good or bad) with the occult – with the body, the landscape, and the über-natural. And as we have seen, the occult-woman is most usually (if not always) associated with the figure of the witch.

In many of the imaginings about Cornwall, the sea is linked to witches, and indeed, witchcraft and Kernow are intrinsically linked: as we have seen, one of the most iconic tourist destinations is the Witchcraft Museum at Boscastle. This fascinating museum places emphasis on the figure of the witch, often in terms of their persecution and the sacrifices they make. This pre-Christian, pagan imagining of the witch translates into a figure that is part of the Cornish landscape – especially the sea. The Witchcraft Museum documents the case of the Pendle witches of Lancashire. These women are forever associated with the infamous hill where they were sacrificed to a fearful, misogynistic, patriarchal, warped Christianity. In contrast, the witches imagined to be associated with Cornwall in our core texts are most often equated with the sea: inherent in this imagining is the figure of the woman or the witch, as embodying the generative: unbounded sexuality, power, and a connection and affinity with both the sea and the moon. In *Ritual*, one of the leading lights of the village, and the richest man there, Laurence Cready says he has his own 'witchcraft museum' (105), typically muddling witchcraft with black magic. He gives Hanlan a tour:

> Once inside the Museum, David quickly scrutinised the contents. Black silk drapes, funereally folded, hung on the black walls. The midnight room had only one window. It was about three feet high and a foot wide in the shape of a Gothic arch. The design of the glass was interesting. A triumphant portrait of Lucifer, with his taloned foot on the nape of Christ's neck. […]
>
> There were purple shelves on the walls filled with purple books. The sign of the Zodiac and the Pentacle were balanced on either side of the window. A black velvet-covered table was placed directly in front of the window, suggesting a portable altar. (105)

This is a deliberate mixing of Folk Horror with the Gothic (perhaps the home of black magic). It should be noted here that in this, we would distinguish between occult practices, black magic, and witchcraft, even if in popular culture – as in *Ritual* – the three are regularly conflated. Although Cready declares to Hanlan after the tour that it is 'all fake' (106), the rest of the novel suggests that while this masculine rendering of the occult might be window dressing, the female-led practices conducted outside in the woods and by the sea are not.

Ritual and *Wicca Woman* are both set in Thorn, a remote (fictional) coastal Cornish village. The outsider, the policeman Hanlan muses, 'When you enter a new country, the old laws are obsolete. And this village is the nearest physical manifestation of fantasy I've ever come across. It has created a new set of rules out of anarchy' (87). The midsummer ritual in Pinner's first novel is in some ways the most brutal. The novel follows the policeman David Hanlan as he attempts to investigate the death of a young girl: Dian Spark. He is thwarted throughout by the villagers themselves, in particular the green-eyed witch, Dian's mother Gwynne, and her highly sexualised young daughter Anna (although this might be Hanlan's construction). Anna is a torment to Hanlan as well as to others and we hear,

> she had gone through men like an enema. Now they considered her to be a whore. She agreed she was. Except she never took money. Perhaps later she would experiment with money. But at the moment she was a hot-house plant and loved it. She realised that she would soon run out of Perfumed Garden exploits. God would be a good experiment to work on next. The Christ God, of course. Her God was here. Her God was different. He was black ice and summer fever. Sulphuric acid could never gnaw him, but he was easy to placate. A little blood and a lot of frenzy and the odd child's innocence. (84)

Despite what Hanlan feels and believes, this is not really anarchy; it is just that (as the tragic character Anna feels) God here is 'different', and this means that the ways of these villagers and the rituals they perform are not Christian ones. Hanlan is confronted with an age-old Midsummer ritual performed by the inhabitants of Thorn: a sea sacrifice where a white horse is slaughtered and a ritual orgy takes place in order to placate the sea and ensure fertility from loins, land, and sea. The narrative of *Ritual* leads up to this frenzied, midsummer pagan ritual:

> The sea pulled them [the villagers] to the circle of Midsummer. Each generation prepared the whole year for this celebration. It was the ritual of blood. Part of their breathing. Even if they wanted to escape the fire in themselves, it would be impossible.
>
> […]
>
> It was the ritual of necessity. The darkness forcing itself into the darkness. The basic earth rhythms of dancing practised secretly in different ways in every country in the world. The dancers, the witch, the goat and the horse, all bound in a circle of urgency to act out themselves. […] Each year the ritual added further dimensions to their lives. It was beautiful because it was natural (158, 162–63).

In this imagining, it is the sea that pulls the Cornish villagers to the ritual (along with echoes of the Bacchae and Frazer). Born into it, there is no escape – it is part of their heritage and part of their very being, naturalised. Thorn's unique secret practice is an embedded part of Cornwall's nature. The villagers cannot help themselves. It is part of their culture and embodied in themselves, their language, and the landscape they reside in.

The ritual builds up to the sacrifice of a horse, after which the village children

> proceeded to decorate the torn head with flowers. Gilly wove willow between its eyes. The twins thrust dogroses into its dead ears. No one spoke as the libation to the sea was completed. Then the labourers dragged the raft to the sea's edge. Slowly the waves laved at the wood, seducing it into the sea. […]
>
> The witch gave thanks. 'For centuries we have done this. Given You and the sea your rites. Give us good harvest and good darkness. Give us' (164).

The fertility rite is to placate the sea. The decorated horse's head is given to the ocean in exchange for bounty. The entire village is involved and while there might be blood, there is in fact balance, as Hanlan recognises:

> The longer [he] stayed in this village, the more he couldn't understand. How could they mix religions like they did? They'd achieved a strange harmony of sadism and laughter, lechery and beauty. He almost envied them. He'd never known anything like it. The nearest thing to it was the Tahitians who practised Voodoo and were also Catholic. In this village in their own secret way, they had found balance (196).

The balance is between the sea and the land, the isolation of the Cornish landscape, and those who inhabit the space. However, we cannot believe Hanlan; although we are paired with him, or at least part of him for most of the book, his words are very far from reliable – he really does not know himself. As befits the hysteria and madness tactics of weird fiction, perhaps all these lurid rites are just his own concoction based on a few mummers and some cider drinking designed to fuel his own perverse, bloody, and ritualistic pleasures. As someone once said, perhaps it was Robin Hardy, you wannabe pagans, be careful what you wish for.

In *Ritual*, and to Hanlan's despair (and perverse delight), Anna's sexuality is excessive, non-Christian, Pagan, and animalistic – a theme Pinner returns to in *The Wicca Woman* where Lulu/Lilith is not separable from her own excessive and overt sexuality. Following even more excessively than intended Mary Whitehouse's injunction against the permissive society, Hanlan sees all sexual desire as disgusting, given voice in the way he describes what he sees; through his Cromwellian guise, he distorts all the indicators of desire into twisted perversity. In this, he is, therefore, a psychotic Hammer of Witches and like Matthew Hopkins libidinally tied into his own logic of transgression, but even as he figures himself as witch hunter, he is also aligned as witch. The sexually active woman in the puritan rhetoric is of course a witch, and it is this that makes Anna subject to Hanlan's desire; we can never be sure that her apparent nymphomania is anything other than Hanlan's fantasy, however. The landlord's daughter in *The Wicker Man* is far more clearly represented as 'bait' for Howie, to test his stoicism and therefore his suitability for sacrifice. Her song and noisy slapping dance that leaves him sweating in his stripey pyjamas have the look of a sexy witch's spell, including movements that could indicate stroking his penis or casting a spell on a poppet. Her confident sexuality chafes against the barrier of his cotton jimjams. She is, however, not quite mistress of her actions; Lord Summerisle appears under her window prior to this, telling her she is the embodiment of the goddess Venus and she is clearly guided by his intentions. *Ritual*'s Anna, of course, also reverses the seduction of the Howie scene played out in *The Wicker Man*, as she ends up murdered by Hanlan, who, like a witch of folklore, uses a bronze pin to kill her, as he did the unfortunate child Billy.

In the article 'Women at Sea', Gemma Goodman, looking at du Maurier's work says, 'the sea is central to the marketing of Cornwall as a tourist site because of its dramatic and aesthetic visual appeal. It can be utilised to emphasise Cornwall's beauty, its wildness and its exoticness' (2016, 175). The imaginings documented here though are not exactly of this sort. The wildness, remoteness, and exoticism might be here, but there is also something else about that which lies underneath – both the granite and the waves. In Pinner's sequel to *Ritual*, the titular *Wicca Woman* is Lilith/Lulu, a supernatural witch-like being who comes to 'save' Thorn. By the time she arrives, 30 years after the events of the first book, it is near the Millennium-eve and a wilder and more elaborate and bloody ritual is being planned. First, three horses are going to be sacrificed, then in increasing frenzy, a man is put on a fire, but he is rescued, and rather like Aslan – in turn a figuration of Christ – in *The Lion, the Witch and the Wardrobe*, Lilith/Lulu (a moon Goddess herself) chooses to sacrifice herself to the sea instead of the intended male victim. Lulu consents to be tied to the cross on which Paul was going to be burnt and urges the villagers to take her down to the sea, 'Because the sea is where I belong' (loc. 5209). And as she floats out across the ocean, she hears a voice: 'Then on the seventh day, I created woman in my own image; so female and then male, I created them both from the earth. But the man failed me. That is why you, Lilith, my first creation, have endless time and tides to bide [...] Especially by the sea' (loc. 5284). It seems that God the redeemer was part pagan after all.

There is no sight of God at all in Susan Cooper's children's novel *Greenwitch*, one of the Dark Is Rising series. Alongside *Over Stone, Under Sea* (1973), the novel is set in Cornwall in Trewissick, another extremely isolated coastal Cornish village (modelled on Mevagissey where Cooper holidayed as a child). Jane, one of the child protagonists, attends an annual women's ritual of the making of the Greenwitch – a female figure constructed over one night in sight of standing stones and from woven wood and leaves – the ritual is connected to the sea goddess Tethys and she is given voice in the story. The Greenwitch is a huge figure crafted by the women of Trewissick every year during a Mayday (Beltane) ritual, woven out of wood: 'Hazel for the framework [...] Rowan for the head. Then the body is of Hawthorne boughs, and Hawthorne blossoms. With the stones within, for the sinking. And those who are crossed, or barren or who would make any wish, must touch the Greenwitch then before she be put to cliff' (45–46). And, as the horse head in *Ritual* is ritualistically fed to the sea on a raft, so this fetishistic figure of the Greenwitch is 'put to cliff' (52) (Figure 14 for an illustrative interpretation of text). At the climax of the Greenwitch ceremony,

> the great green tree-woven figure of the Greenwitch [...] was flung out into the air and down over the end of Kemare Head. For a split second it was there, visible, falling, in the blue and the green among the wheeling screaming white gulls, and then it was gone, plunging down, driven by the weight of the stones inside its body. There was a silence as if all Cornwall held its breath, and then they heard the splash (55).

In this ritual, the *Greenwitch* is given back to the sea – and this is where she resides. As a central plot node in the story, Jane feels the Greenwitch's loneliness and hears her voice; Greenwitch is not just an idol, but an ancient, sentient animated being who lives deep in the ocean. Jane dreams of the Greenwitch under the sea:

> The whole structure swayed now and then, rhythmically, when the long reach of the stormswell pulled at it.
>
> Then as Jane watched, the swaying grew more pronounced, as though the storm were reaching deeper into the sea. [...] Jane felt a dark chill in the water, a sense of great threatening power, and to her horror the movement of the Greenwitch changed. Limbs stirred of themselves, the leafy head rippled and stirred as if it were a face [...] now the Greenwitch, she knew, was alive. It was neither good nor evil, it was simply alive (72–74).

In these imaginings of Cornish rituals, the sea becomes a living presence that is not only beneficent and fertile but also life-taking and terrible. As well as the land, the sea is an othered realm, hostile yet providing.

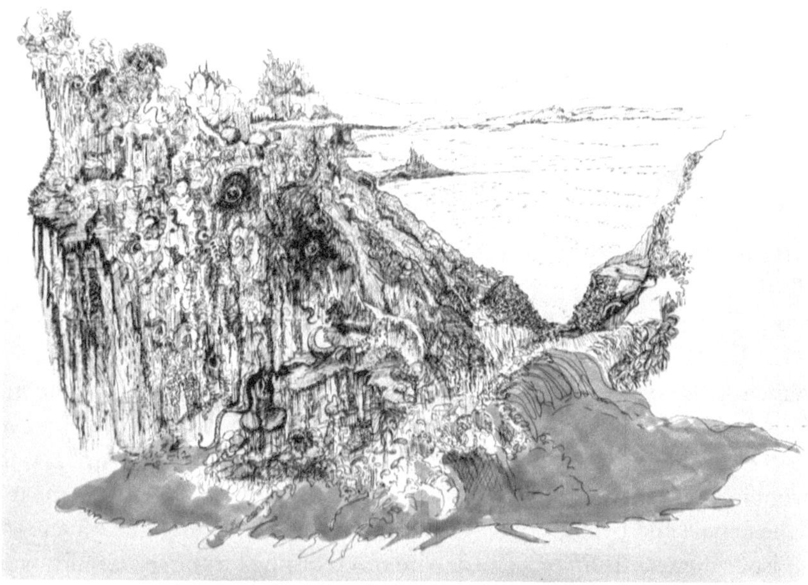

Figure 14 The site of Jane's initiation in Susan Cooper's *The Greenwitch. The Gribben Head* by Tanya Krzywinska (2021). Ink on paper.

Scovell writes,

> The British relationship with landscape is a complex one that is intertwined within the history of its artistic practice, and Folk Horror builds heavily upon this practice by sitting obtusely within its context, simultaneously turning it on its head. [...] Folk horror finds much within the initial ideas of Romanticism, especially in its admiration and use of landscape, but it instead forcibly uses its anti-rationalist disregard for Enlightenment thinking in various extreme ways to show an inherent danger in such self-indulgent abandon' (37).

The Folk Horror texts examined here take this further (in fact out into the sea) and engage, with constructive creativeness, with the slippages between the non-and-pre-Christian and the untameable, the savage, and the truly wild. In doing so, contra Scovell, these Cornish-Gothic, Cornish-Folk Horror texts redeem the Pagan and the Romantic and perhaps even the self-indulgent. The Cornish landscape invites indulgence while at the same time, the underlying black granite repels complete immersion. Perhaps the way 'in' to this landscape *has* to be ritualised and the sea, which has more power than the land, propitiated.

Recently, Jimmy Packham has examined Wyl Menmuir's Gothic tale which is set in a Cornish fishing village, *The Many*. Here, as entropy envelops the sea, its bounty, the village, and its inhabitants, fishing has become 'ritual rather than function' (2016, 213). Menmuir's novel can certainly be equated with Folk Horror, but in a way, it is the absence or erosion of belief (particularly in the sea itself) that characterises the horror. For the texts examined here, the rituals are elaborately constructed and designed to propitiate the sea. Lilith/Lulu's own sea sacrifice will put an end to the sacrifices because, as the Witch Gwynne tells the men, 'the harvests will just have to be what they'll be. [...] You see, so far, all your sacrificial fires have achieved nothing but endless suffering' (loc 5242). In *The Wicker Man*, the sacrifice is of fire and made to address the sun (named as the Irish sun deity Nuada by Summerisle); similarly, the sacrifice the men of Thorn were baying for in *Wicca Woman* was also for fire; however, it is the sea that presides in those Folk Horror fictions set in Cornwall. It is the fecundity and otherness of the sea that prevails and is connected in some way to the female and feminine power. For Pinner, this is evident in the way that he eroticises the sea. In *Ritual* we hear, 'the sun is lusting for the sea. Squirting his liquid amber, he hears the submarine call for the mermen and the Kraken. The upper air vibrates like a sheet of crystal as the sun plunges into the water. One long hiss of pain and the water devours the fire. There is only the perfection of darkness' (84). In Cornwall, it is the sea that envelopes and defeats the solar fire. Greater than the flames, the ocean demands respect. In *The Wicker Man*, the sun looks on bright and oblivious to Summerisle's offerings, and indeed to Howie's agony, this sun is not the Nuada of Irish myth, who is meant to be honourable and righteous. One is left with a sense of the sun's terrible implacability and this is underlined by Howie's prediction that next year, the King must die for the cycle of sacrifice to perpetuate. Yet, in the Cornish rituals and where the rituals and the sacrifices are to the sea, it is the women who lead the watery way and, instead of pessimism, we see bounty and a conception of the Other as life-affirming.

CONCLUSION

This book was conceived and written during the 2020 COVID-19 pandemic. Cornwall was seen as a place of refuge by fearful city dwellers and anxieties grew as tourists flocked to the region. Social media posts from holidaymakers and residents showed wide open spaces, glorious seascapes, 'empty' beaches, and towering cliffs. This recreation of Cornwall is the newest addition to centuries of imagining Cornwall as special and strange. There are the wildly romantic landscapes, the stones standing as markers of a far distant but very present past, the sense of both escape and entrapment, and, of course, in all this the dark side: the unwelcome outsiders, the glowering locals, the gap between rich and power, the undercurrent of violence, and the dark dangers writ into the landscape itself. It is this imagining of Cornwall that sustains a continued dialogue with the generic Gothic. When we conceived of this book, the strength of the role that Cornwall has played in the making of the Gothic was not fully apparent to us. Kernow has served the Gothic as inspiration and as a mise en scène of dark desire, from its generative role in the development of Folk Horror through to a brand of melodrama that has become the siren-song of Gothic romanticism. These modes stretch across different forms, genres, and platforms, from children's fiction to fine art practice and poetry, through to dark tourism. Who knew that Cornwall was the crucible out of which so much strange fiction was born?

As a place rural, wild and seemingly lying outside of urban time, Cornwall is usefully described in Gothic romantic terms through the concept of *Genius Loci* (spirit of place). As Alexander Pope (1731) puts it:

> Consult the genius of the place in all;
> That tells the waters to rise, or fall;
> Or helps th' ambitious hill the heav'ns to scale,
> Or scoops in circling theatres the vale;
> Calls in the country, catches opening glades,
> Joins willing woods, and varies shades from shades,
> Now breaks, or now directs, th' intending lines;
> Paints as you plant, and, as you work, designs
> (Epistle IV, to Richard Boyle, Earl of Burlington)

Genius Loci demands a subtle receptivity to the topographic as it presents itself at a given moment, calling on both intention and imagination. The late Victorian traveller and author of supernatural stories Vernon Lee describes the sentiment of the 'genius of the landscape' thus:

> although what I call the *Genius Loci* can never be personified, we may yet feel him nearer and more potent, in some individual monument of feature of the landscape. He is immanent very often, and subduing our hearts most deeply, at a given turn of a road; or a path cut in terraces in a hillside, with view of great distant mountains; [...] most of all, perhaps, in the meeting-place of streams, or the mouth of a river. [...] The genius of places lurks there; or, more strictly, he is it. (1898, 6)

An anthropomorphic approach is by nature animistic: place becomes alive through our emotional and imaginative engagement. This is what underpins so much of the Gothic, a visceral, lived response to the strangeness of place. It is in Pinner's *Ritual* as much as in Colquhoun's subtle art practices. The Gothic provides a set of coordinates for seeing a specific topology in such a way as to bring out its dark and secret otherworldliness.

Ritual responds to that otherworldliness, appealing to it, appalled by it, celebrating it. But it is a text that is conflicted in its relationship to animism. By contrast, Peter Grey's 'Rewilding Witchcraft' asks us to approach pagan ritual through an unselfish anthropomorphism, putting place before personal desire. He says, 'Ours is a practice grounded in the land, in the web of spirit relationships, in plant and insect and animal and bird. This is where we need to orient our actions, this is where our loyalty lies' (36).

Grey talks about the land, however, Cornwall is very much about the sea. In the strange fictions about Cornwall, the witching women of Cornwall – the sea witches – are prepared to sacrifice a great deal for the communities they live in and the place they occupy. Representations of ritual in the context of Gothic often hint at this unselfish sacrifice, although often it is sensationalism that drowns this affirmation out. However, in many of the generative rituals enacted in Cornwall, place takes precedence over the individual and the forces of *Genius Loci* appealed to, placated at least for a while.

The Cornish landscapes are barely those of mainland England. Cornwall is always never-quite England, and this marginality has as we have seen played a leading role in its Gothic representations. Cornwall's terrain and materiality continue to signify as an outsider space, with its lost lands, eccentrics, witches old and new, Celtic saints, and its folk traditions as remnants of pagan cultures remaindered by Christianisation. All this has fueled the Gothic imaginations of writers, artists, and performers, as well as pagans, witches, and magicians. What we are left with, then, is the persistence of animistic and generative forces that call us back into the dark ages. Aelfric, an Anglo-Saxon monk writing in the 900s, calls us to the Christian creed away from such heathen preoccupations and practices; frustrated with the persistence of the old ways, he writes,

> Some men are so blinded that they bring their offerings to an earth-fast stone, and also to the trees, and to well springs, even as witches teach, and will not understand how foolishly they act, or how the dead stone or the dumb tree can help them or give them health. (cited in Bates 2002, 106)

In citing Aelfric, Brian Bates implies that Aelfric's apparent rationalism chimes with that of our culture, 'Today, in the high-tech Western world, we are far more distanced from the sources of our sustenance, and do not therefore feel so attuned to its precious regeneration.' (2002, 131). He refers here to what he calls 'wells of wisdom', referring specifically to Sancreed Well, designed in such a way to allow people to bathe in located in West Penwith. Bates claims that such ancient wells provided a conduit for connecting Celts and Anglo-Saxons to the Otherworld, that they represented the well-spring of life and were sites where women came to perform fertility magic. Our connection with that otherworld has been all but lost, he says; however, if you were to go to Sancreed Well today, you would see many small offerings and tattered cloths tied to the nearby thorn bushes. Our estrangement from an animist otherworld is, therefore, not fully sealed. In the Gothic imagination, we see a continued and uncanny exchange between the human world and the forces of nature. Given the insistence of the climate crisis, this conversation is not something to be dismissed as antique novelty and sensationalism, instead has become loaded with fears about our future as a species. Kernow's rural Gothic is, therefore, more cogent than ever. Not only does it find purchase in critical questions around seeing nature as simply a 'resource' for the benefit of 'mankind', but it is also informed by an impetus to regain a life-enhancing sense of connection with place, its *Genius Loci.* That is why this book's authors, both incomers from the urban sprawl, live in Cornwall, and in that and in the writing of this book we acknowledge that, like du Maurier, Colquhoun, and Pinner, we are instrumental in perpetuating its myth as a place of deep and subtle magics. We hope that our book has shown that an animist magical conversation is still very much alive and present in the Gothic cast given to Cornwall and in its strange fictions.

WORKS CITED

Aloi, Peg. 2016. 'Robin Hardy, Director of Iconic Pagan Film THE WICKER MAN, Has Died'. 2 July. Accessed 14 January 2020. https://www.patheos.com/blogs/themediawitches/2016/07/robin-hardy-director-of-iconic-pagan-film-the-wicker-man-has-died/.

Aristotle. n.d. 'Aristotle on Tragedy'. 'Selection from the Poetics of Aristotle'. Accessed 1 December 2020.

Baker, Phil. 2015. 'Dennis Wheatley'. In *The Occult World.* Christopher Partridge (ed.), 464–68. New York: Routledge.

Bates, Brian. 2002. *The Real Middle Earth: Magic and Mystery in the Dark Ages.* Basingstoke, Oxford: Pan Macmillan.

Bauduin, Tessel M. 2015. 'The Occult and the Visual Arts'. In *The Occult World.* Christopher Partridge (ed.), 429–45. London: Routledge.

Beauman, Sally. 2007. 'My Cousin Rachel'. In *The Daphne Du Maurier Companion.* Helen Taylor (ed.), 47–60. London: Virago Press.

Bell, Catherine. 1992. Ritual Theory, Ritual Practice. Oxford: Oxford University Press.

Botting, Fred, and Justin D. Edwards. 2013. 'Theorising Global Gothic'. In *Globalgothic.* Glennis Byron (ed.), 1124. Manchester: Manchester University Press.

Bottrell, William. 1870. *Traditions and Hearthside Stories of West Cornwall, First Series.* Penzance: W. Cornish.

———. 1873. *Traditions and Hearthside Stories of West Cornwall, Second Series.* Penzance: Beare and Son.

———. 1880. *Stories and Folk-Lore of West Cornwall, Third Series.* Penzance: F. Rodda.

Brown, Allan. 2000. *Inside the Wicker Man: The Morbid Ingenuities.* Edinburgh: Sidgwick and Jackson.

Browning, Christian. 1992. 'Introduction'. In *Vanishing Cornwall.* Daphne du Maurier, 5–8. Harmondsworth: Penguin.

Burkert, Walter. 1983. *Homo Necans: The Anthropology of Ancient Greek Sacrificial Ritual and Myth.* Translated by Peter Bing. Berkley: University of California Press.

———. 1985. *Greek Religion.* Translated by John Raffan. Oxford: Blackwell.

Busby, Mattha. 2021. 'Carbis Bay in Cornwall to Host G7 Summit in June'. 16 January. https://www.theguardian.com/uk-news/2021/jan/16/carbis-bay-in-cornwall-to-host-g7-summit-in-june. Accessed 12 July 2021.

Byron, Glennis. 2013. *Globalgothic.* Manchester: Manchester University Press.

Caillois, Roger. 2001. *Man, Play and Games.* Translated by Meyer Barash. Urbana: University of Illinois Press.

Caputo, J. 2001. *On Religion.* London: Routledge.

Collins, Willkie. 1851. *Rambles Beyond Railways; Or, Notes in Cornwall Taken A-Foot.* London: Richard Bentley.

Colquhoun, Ithell. 2003. *The Goose of Hermogenes.* London: Peter Owen.

———2007. In *The Magical Writings of Ithell Colquhoun.* Steve Nicholls (ed.), n.p.

———. 2016. *The Living Stones.* London: Peter Owen.

———. 2019. In *Medea's Charms.* Richard Shillitoe (ed.). London: Peter Owen.

Cooper, Susan. 1974. *Greenwitch.* London: Red Fox.

Cox, Jess. 2019. *Neo-Victorianism and Sensation Fiction.* Basingstoke: Palgrave Macmillan.

Crowley, Aleister. 1987. *777 and Other Qabalistic Writings of Aleister Crowley.* London: Red Wheel.

Dalton, Stephen. 2019. 'Bait Review'. *The Hollywood Reporter*, February.

Danchev, Alex. 2011. *100 Artists' Manifestos: From the Futurists to the Stuckists.* Harmondsworth: Penguin.

Deleuze, Gilles, and Felix Guattri. 1980. *A Thousand Plateaus.* Minneapolis: University of Minnesota Press.

Doyle, Arthur Conan. 1907. *Through the Magic Door.* Classic Literature Library. https://classic-literature.co.uk/scottish-authors/arthur-conan-doyle/through-the-magicdoor/ebook-page-22.asp. Accessed 5 July 2021.

Du Maurier, Daphne. 1951/2017. *My Cousin Rachel.* London: Virago Press.

———. 1989. *Enchanted Cornwall.* London: Michael Joseph.

———. 1992. *Vanishing Cornwall.* Harmondsworth: Penguin.

———2011.' East Wind' in The Doll: Short Stories. London: Virago.

———. 2012. *Vanishing Cornwall.* London: Virago Press.

Dunn, Jamie. 2019. 'Mark Jenkin on Bait'. *The Skinny: Independent Cultural Journalism*, 26, August.

Durkheim, Émile. 1995. *The Elementary Forms of Religious Life.* Translated by Karen E. Fields. New York: Free Press.

Dyer, Richard. 1981. 'Entertainment and Utopia'. In *Genre: The Musical – a Reader*, Rick Altman (ed.), 175–89. London: RKP with BFI.

Franks, Benjamin, Stephen Harper, Jonathan Murray, and Lesley Stevenson. 2006. *The Quest for the Wicker Man: History, Folklore and Pagan Perspectives.* Edinburgh: Luath Press.

Frazer, James, George. 1994. *The Golden Bough: A Study in Magic and Religion. A New Abridgement from the Second and Third Editions.* Robert Fraser (ed.). Oxford: Oxford University Press.

Freud, Sigmund. 1990. 'Totem and Taboo'. In *The Origins of Religion, Volume 13 The Penguin Freud Library.* Albert Dickson (ed.). Translated by James Strachey, 43–224. Harmondsworth: Penguin Books.

Gardner, Gerald B. 1988. *The Meaning of Witchcraft: The Mystery of Life.* New York: Magickal Childe.

Gary, Gemma. 2019. *Traditional Witchcraft: A Cornish Book of Ways.* Cornwall: Troy Books.

Gluckman, Max. 1965. *Politics, Law and Ritual in Tribal Societies.* Aldine: Chicago University Press.

Godwin, Kerriann (ed.). 2012. *The Museum of Witchcraft: A Magical History.* Boscastle: The Occult Art Company.

Goodman, Gemma. 2016. 'Women at Sea: Locating and Escaping Gender on the Cornish Coast in Daphne du Maurier's *The Loving Spirit* and *Frenchman's Creek*'. In *Sea Narratives: Cultural Responses to the Sea, 1600–Present.* Charlotte Mathieson (ed.). London: Palgrave.

Grey, Peter. 2019. 'Rewilding Witchcraft'. In *The Brazen Vessel*, Alkistis Dimech and Grey Peter (eds), 34–47. London: Scarlet Imprint.

Hale, Amy. 2020. *Ithell Colquhoun: Genius of the Fern Loved Gully.* London: Strange Attractor.

Hale, Amy. 2004. 'The Land Near the Dark Cornish Sea: The Development of Tintagel as a Celtic Pilgrimmage Site'. *Journal for the Academic Study of Magic* (2): 206–25.

Hale, Amy. 2012. 'The Magical Life of Ithell Colquhoun'. In *Pathways in Modern Western Magic* by Nevill Drury. Richmond, CA: Conscrescent Scholars.

Hardy, Robin, and Anthony Shaffer. 2000. *The Wicker Man: A Novel of Religious Sexuality and Pagan Murder.* Basingstoke: Pan Books.

Heholt, Ruth. 2018. 'The Hammer House of Cornish Horror: The Inversion of Imperial Gothic in *The Plague of the Zombies* and *The Reptile*'. In *Gothic Britain: Dark Places in the Provinces and Margins of the British Isles*, 195–210. Cardiff: University of Wales Press.

Horner, Avril, and Sue Zlosnik. 1998. *Daphne du Maurier: Writing, Identity and the Gothic Imagination.* Basingstoke: MacMillan Press.

Howells, Coral Ann. 2007. 'Canadian Gothic'. In *The Routledge Companion to Gothic.* Catherine and Emma McEvoy Spooner (eds), 105–14. Abingdon: Routledge.

Hughes, William, and Ruth Heholt. (eds). 2018. *Gothic Britain: Dark Places in the Provinces and the Margins of the British Isles.* Cardiff: University of Wales Press.

Hughes, William. 2020. 'Foreword: On the Gothic Nature of Gardens'. In *Ecogothic Gardens in the Long Nineteenth Century: Phantoms, Fantasy and Uncanny Flowers.* Sue Edney (ed.), xiv–xvii. Manchester: Manchester University Press.

Hunt, Robert F. R. S., 1865. *Popular Romances of the West of England; or The Drolls, Traditions and Superstitions of Old Cornwall, First Series.* London: John Camden Hotten.

Huizinga, Johannes. 1949. *Homo Ludens: A Study of the Play-Element in Culture.* London: Routledge & Kegan Paul.

Keetley, Dawn. 2020. 'Introduction'. In 'Folk Horror' issue, Dawn Keetley (ed.), *Revenant: Critical and Creative Studies of the Supernatural*, no. 5: 1–32.

Kermode, Mark, in conversation with Mark Jenkin. 2019. Commentary on *Bait.* 2019. Directed by Mark Jenkin. Performed by Early Days Films.

Kiang, Jessica. 2019. *Commentary Book for 'Bait'.* London: British Film Institute.

Killeen, Jarlath. 2009. *History of the Gothic: Gothic Literature 1825–1914.* Cardiff: University of Wales Press.

Lee, Vernon. 1898. *Genius Loci: Notes on Places.* Chicago: Leopold Classic Library.

Lehtonen, Mikko. 2000. *The Cultural Analysis of Texts.* London: Sage.

Lepetit, Patrick. 2012. *The Esoteric Secrets of Surrealism.* Rochester: Inner Traditions.

Lee, Vernon. 1898. *Genius Loci: Notes on Places.* Chicago: Leopold Classic Library.

Mantgani, Ian. 2019. 'Bait First Look: Mark Jenkin Heralds the New Weird Britain'. *Sight and Sound*, 30 August.

Matthews, Caitlin. 1990. *Voices of the Goddess: A Chorus of Sibyls.* Northampton: Aquarian Press.

Menmuir, Wyl. 2016. *The Many.* Cromer: Salt.

Michell, David. 2017. 'Commentary'. *My Cousin Rachel.* Fox Searchlight Pictures.

Michell, David (dir.). 2017. *My Cousin Rachel.*

Mighall, Robert. 2003. *A Geography of Victorian Gothic Fiction: Mapping History's Nightmares.* Oxford: Oxford University Press.

Mishra, Vijay. 2012. 'The Gothic Sublime'. In *A New Companion to the Gothic.* David Punter (ed.), 288–306. Oxford: John Wiley & Sons.

Mosely, Rachel. 2013. 'Women at the Edge: Encounters with the Cornish Coast in British Film and Television'. *Continuum: Journal of Media and Cultural Studies* 27 (5): 644–62.

Murphy, Bernice. 2022 'Black Boxes and Corn: Backwoods Horror and Human Sacrifice in American Folk Horror Narratives'. In *Folk Horror: New Global Pathways*. Dawn Keetley and Ruth Heholt (eds). Cardiff: University of Wales Press.

Murray, Margaret Alice. 2019. *The Witch-Cult in Western Europe*. London: Aziloth Books.

Neve, Christopher. 2020. *Unquiet Landscape*. London: Thames and Hudson.

Packham, Jimmy. 2018. 'The Gothic Coast: Boundaries, Belonging, and Coastal Community in Contemporary British Fiction'. *Critique: Studies in Contemporary Fiction* 205–21. Accessed 20 December 2020. doi:https://www.tandfonline.com/doi/abs/10.1080/00111619.2018.1524744?journalCode=vcrt20.

Packer, Joseph, and Ethan Stoneman. 2018. *A Feeling of Wrongness: Pessimistic Rhetoric on the Fringes of Popular Culture*. Philadelphia: Pennsylvania University Press.

Partridge, Christopher (ed.). 2015. 'The Occult and Popular Music'. In *The Occult World*. 531–38. London: Routledge.

——— (ed.). 2015. *The Occult World*. London: Routledge.

Pinner, David. 2011. *Ritual*. Finders Keepers.

———. 2014. *Wicca Woman*. Lume Books. Accessed 1 December 2020. Kindle version.

Pope, Alexander, 1731. 'Epistle IV, to Richard Boyle, Earl of Burlington'. Accessed 8 February 2021. 'https://www.poetryfoundation.org/poems/44894/epistles-to-several-persons-epistle-iv.

Ratcliffe, Eric. 2007/2016. *Ithell Colquhoun: Pioneer Surrealist, Artist, Occultist, Writer and Poet*. Oxford: Mandrake of Oxford.

Redgrove, Peter. 1987. *The Black Goddess and the Sixth Sense*. London: Paladin.

Scovell, Adam. 2017. *Folk Horror: Hours Dreadful and Things Strange*. Leighton Buzzard: Auteur.

Shillitoe, Richard. 2009. *Ithell Colquhoun: Magician Born of Nature*. London: Lulu Press.

Shuttle, Penelope, and Peter Redgrove. 1978. *The Wise Wound*. Harmondsworth: Penguin.

Sky News. 2021. 'Cornwall Seaside Resort to Host G7 Summit of World Leaders'. 16 January. https://news.sky.com/story/carbis-bay-in-cornwall-chosen-to-host-this-years-g7-summit-12190119. Accessed 20 February 2021.

Smith, Dan, E. 2019. 'Modern Ghosts of the Coast: "Bait", "The Lighthouse", and Contemporary Thresholds'. The Medium: Accessed 2 December 2020. https://medium.com/@godardorgohome/modern-ghosts-of-the-coast-bait-the-lighthouse-and-contemporary-thresholds-957f58d4a38d.

Spare, Austin. 2005. *The Book of Automatic Drawing*. I-H-O Books.

Spooner, Catherine, and Emma McEvoy. 2009. *The Routledge Companion to Gothic*. London: Routledge.

Stanley, Bob. 2011. 'Introduction'. In David Pinner. *Ritual*. Finders Keepers.

Stephenson, Barry. 2011. *Ritual: A Very Short Introduction*. Oxford: Oxford University Press.

Swancutt, Katherine. 2019. *Animism*. Accessed 12 November 2020. doi:http://doi.org/10.29164/19anim.

Trower, Shelley. 2015. *Rocks of Nation: The Imagination of Celtic Cornwall*. Manchester: Manchester University Press.

Turner, Victor. 1982. *From Ritual to Theatre: The Human Seriousness of Play*. New York: PAJ.

van Elferen, Isabella. 2013. 'Fantasy music: epic soundtracks, magical instruments, musical metaphysics'. *Journal of the Fantastic in the Arts*, 24 (2): 4–24.

Walters, Kate. 2011. *Mysterious Tissue: Of Flesh and Stars*. Millennium.

The Wicker Man. 1973. Director Robert Hardy. British Lion Film Corporation.

Westland, Ella. 1995. 'The Passionate Periphery: Cornwall and Romantic Fiction'. In *Peripheral Visions: Images of Nationhood in Contemporary British Fiction.* Ian A. Bell (ed.), 153–72. Cardiff: University of Wales Press.

Westland, Ella. 2007. 'The View from Kilmarth: Daphne du Maurier's Cornwall'. In *The Daphne du Maurier Companion*, Helen Taylor (ed.), 114–21. London: Virago Press.

White, Rupert. 2017. *The Enchanted Landscape: Earth Mysteries, Paganism & Art in Cornwall 1950–2000.* Antenna.

INDEX

www.ingramcontent.com/pod-product-compliance
Lightning Source LLC
LaVergne TN
LVHW050938080826
845145LV00004B/1314

* 9 7 8 1 7 8 5 2 7 9 0 6 5 *